THE HISTORY OF THE
PENNSYLVANIA
RAILROAD

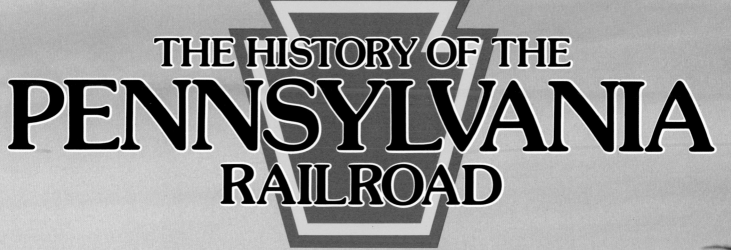

THE HISTORY OF THE
PENNSYLVANIA
RAILROAD

TIMOTHY JACOBS

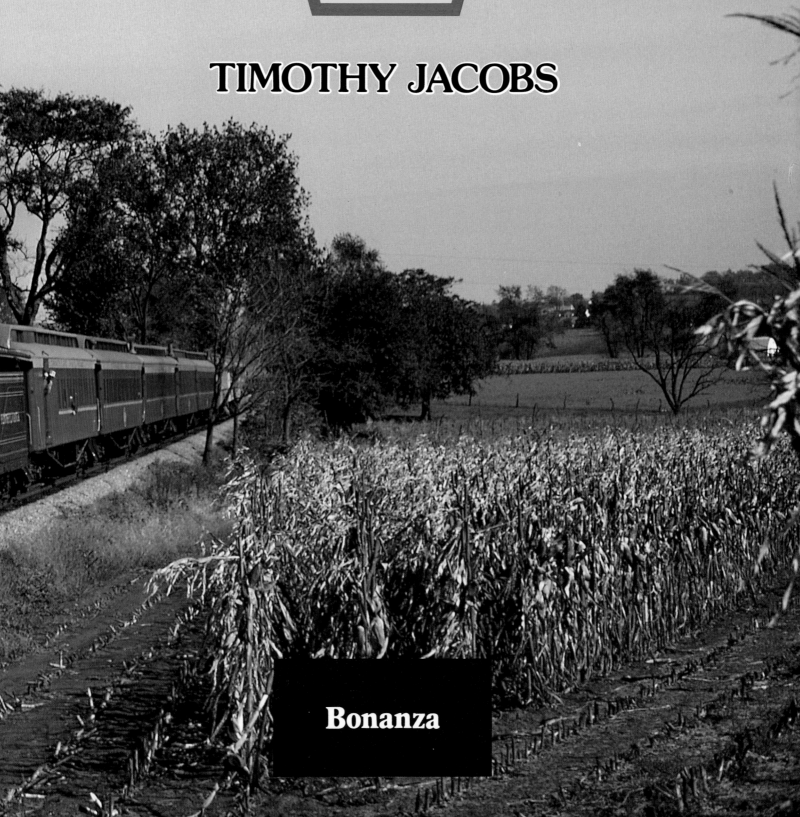

Bonanza

Published 1988 by
Bonanza Books, distributed by
Crown Publishers Inc.

Produced by Brompton Books Corp.
15 Sherwood Place
Greenwich, CT 06830, USA

Printed in Hong Kong

ISBN 0-517-63351-5

h g f e d

PHOTO CREDITS

Amtrak 118
Association of American Railroads 10–11, 14–15, 19 (top right), 26–27, 35, 62, 63, 64
Bison Books 1, 124
California State Railroad Museum 38, 41, 42–43, 48–49, 53, 55, 56–57, 59, 65, 66 (top), 67, 78–79, 82, 85, 86, 88, 89, 93, 97, 104, 112–113
Charles A Brown 8–9, 29, 36, 71, 106–107, 109
Conrail 116–117, 120
Currier & Ives 6–7, 22–23
General Electric 74, 75, 111
George Hamlin 119, 122
HL Broadbelt 16–17, 18–19, 31, 32–33, 46, 60–61, 66 (bottom), 68–69, 73, 77, 100–101
PHMC Railroad Museum of Pennsylvania 76
Southern Pacific Historical Collection 13 (bottom)
Steamscenes 2–3, 90–91, 95, 110, 114–115, 126–127
Stevens Institute of Technology 13 (top right)

Designed by Tom Debolski

Edited by Pamela Berkman

Captioned by Timothy Jacobs

ACKNOWLEDGEMENTS

The author would like to thank Charles Brown of the New Haven Railroad Historical and Technical Association for his swift and excellent assistance; Pamela Berkman for her invaluable assistance; and his grandfather Lee McClelland Duffield—Pennsy man and *raconteur*.

Page 1: Two Pennsylvania Railroad K4s Pacific 4–6–2s face the camera, and an M1a freight locomotive is apparent at extreme photo left. The K4s was *the* Pennsy passenger hauler in the last days of steam, though the hard-charging E6s Atlantic was 'right up there.'

Pages 2-3: Design precursors of the E6s 4–4–2, two vintage E3d Atlantics hustle a passenger train through the Carpenters, Pennsylvania landscape on a museum exhibition run in 1983.

These pages: Coupled back-to-back, the electric cab unit locomotives shown here symbolize the extensive electrification projects which the Pennsy undertook in the 20th century. Such units as these General Electric locos produced up to 4000hp apiece.

CONTENTS

INTRODUCTION

The dust has settled, and the railroad with the familiar keystone logo is all but memory now. The largest railroad in the world for most of its 121-year lifespan, the most part of its mighty skeleton now forms the foundation for that modern titan, Conrail, which operates in 15 states and two Canadian provinces. The history of the keystone state is very much a part of the history of the railroad that bore the keystone logo, for the rise and fall of the Pennsy in large part also depended upon the possibilities of a regional way of thinking.

Comprising over 10,000 miles of operated track at its height, and compounding that trackage by use of the Pennsy's hallmark four tracking system, the Pennsy moved more freight and more passengers than any other railroad in the world. Those broad thoroughfares of steel gleamed like the envy in the eyes of the grand road's competitors as the Pennsy's huge 20th century locomotives thundered in seeming endless succession with their long, long trains of groaning cars behind them.

From the luxury of the Pennsy's famous *Broadway Limited,* which mounted its supremacy over the New York Central's *20th Century Limited* behind the huge and super fast E6s Atlantic and K4 Pacific locomotives, to the unbelievable expanse of the huge freight yard at Enola, the Pennsy, with its peak rolling stock of nearly 7000 locomotives and 282,000-plus cars of all kinds in 1929 was simply overwhelming in its complexity, grandeur, and singularity.

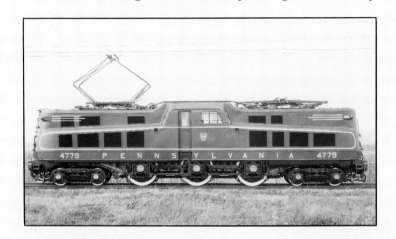

Some deemed it poetic justice when, in 1968, the Pennsy's merger was completed with its old and always eager rival, the New York Central. From the early 1830s when the Erie Canal first trumpeted the news that New York, and not Philadelphia, would be the queen of US commerce, to the days when the two roads' crack passenger trains would come flashing out of Chicago on close-set, parallel tracks, the two roads were extensions of the regional way of thought of the great industrial Northeast, which would be dealt heavy blows in the 1960s and 1970s.

When one remembers a grandfather who was a brakeman on the Pennsy, his tales of heroism and tragedy on the great road still give added dimension to the sight of a large freight threading its way through those green and round-shouldered eastern mountains.

So the time and the glory and memories come and go; from the *John Bull* to the *Metroliner;* from wood to coal to electric to diesel fuel; the impetus to recall those days when the keystone number plate rode upon the nose of many a huge-boilered freight engine is still powerful. The hiss of steam; a throbbing diesel; the cantankerous clank of an old time handcar—this and much, much more was the Pennsy.

Previous pages: Nineteenth century railroading according to Currier & Ives. As well as deriving its name and being from the Keystone State, the Pennsy saw itself as—and it was—the keystone of US railroading. *Below:* A huge Pennsy 2-10-4 J1 freight loco heads a train near the tunnel at Gallitzin—one of the original stretches of track built by the Pennsylvania Railroad—in 1946. The J1 and its tender weighed 987,380 lbs. Inset photo: A 'steeple cab' P-5A electric, in 1934.

BEGINNINGS

Robert Stevens

In 1830, Robert L Stevens, son of shipping and horse-railroad baron John Stevens, set sail for England to buy a locomotive and rails for his father's Camden & Amboy Railroad.

During the trip, Stevens whittled various models of what seemed to him to be a viable rail configuration. Up to the moment Stevens perfected what, in cross-section, looked like an inverted letter 'T', railroads in the United States were rolling on a variety of rails, the most common being made of strips of wood topped with flat strips of iron, set down on a roadbed comprised of stones—so that the rail cars would be prevented from sinking into the ground when passing over the rails with a full load.

The main disadvantage of this arrangement was that the flat iron strips sometimes came loose from the wood and either derailed the cars, tangled in their wheels or punched through the car bottoms, injuring passengers, and sometimes injured the horses which were commonly used to draw the cars. Robert Stevens wanted to create a practical alternative to this kind of faulty equipment. He also had a mission to seek out a reliable, working locomotive. One of these objectives was realized by the time he set foot on British soil—he'd more or less perfected the shape of the first true iron railroad rail.

Stevens persuaded Guest, Lewis and Company of Dowlais, Wales to roll him some rail. The new rail was a success when it was delivered to the US, and soon enough, the demand for iron rail on the part of the railroads in general necessitated the domestic production of Stevens' invention. Toward this end, the Montour Rolling Mill was set up at Danville, Pennsylvania in 1845, and began producing the 'T' rail in quantity.

Robert Stevens was the son of Colonel John Stevens, one of the earliest American proponents of steam locomotive power, who had even built a model railroad, complete with steam locomotive, on his estate in New Jersey. Stevens himself owned boats, but as a proponent of steam railroad power, he had sent his son Robert, in the capacity of the head of Camden & Amboy, to buy the best locomotive that England had to offer. Railways had been operative for some time in Great Britain—the industrial revolution having gotten a bit of a head start there—with the US playing 'catch up.'

John Bull

Robert Stevens went to the Stephenson Works, where he witnessed the trials of their locomotive called *Planet*. Sufficiently impressed by the cantankerous, internally-linked little engine, he ordered a copy made for the Camden & Amboy, to be shipped at the earliest date. Robert Stevens' new engine was dubbed *John Bull*, in honor of its British birthplace.

The engine was shipped in one piece, save for a few trifles—the rods, pistons, wheels and other vital parts were packed in their own little boxes, and there were no instructions regarding their assembly. A young mechanic saved the day.

When *John Bull* arrived at Philadelphia in August 1831, Isaac Dripps, employed by the Stevens Company as a mechanic on their steamboat line that plied the Mississippi, met the boat. Dripps was charged with the task of putting *John Bull* together. Neither Dripps nor the Stevenses, father and son, could have fully conceived what their little smoke belcher would beget.

Matthias Baldwin

This same type of engine, in the form of hasty, ill-defined sketches brought back from the Rainhill locomotive trials in Great Britain, would provide the model for Matthias Baldwin's first locomotive. Baldwin was a former watchmaker, who had turned to manufacturing stationary industrial steam engines as a sideline. Soon the industrial steam engine business became so lucrative that Baldwin went into it wholesale.

Public interest in locomotives had been aroused by reports from overseas regarding the regular use of steam locomotives in passenger service by the British. Franklin Peale, proprietor of the Philadelphia Museum, felt that an exhibit at his establishment might prove to be very popular. Peale went to see Baldwin, whose steam engines had established a very good reputation for their ingenuity and reliability. Peale had in his possession sketches of the *Planet/John Bull* class locomotive; he wanted Baldwin to build a miniature locomotive—sufficient to haul a few passengers—for his exhibit.

The exhibition took place within the walls of the museum. Tracks were constructed of barrel-hoop iron nailed to pine boards, and the train consisted of the miniature locomotive and two four-passenger cars. The engine was coal-fueled and its exhaust was routed through the Museum's chimney. The exhibit was a whopping success, and throngs of visitors crowded the museum to witness and participate in what would eventually turn out to be a prophetic event: the city of Philadelphia and its citizens' worldly commerce would give birth in just a little more than a decade to the Pennsylvania Railroad.

On 12 November 1831, *John Bull* hauled its first passengers—members of the New Jersey state legislature—on a small test track in Bordentown. The train consisted of two stagecoach-style cars which were built by MP and ME Green of Hoboken. Shortly after this, Matthias Baldwin came by to inspect *John Bull*, and the Stevenses, sensing a possible source of domestically built locomotives, graciously let him do so.

What neither Baldwin nor the Stevenses knew was that they were forging the foundation for the mightiest railroad of them all.

Old Ironsides

Baldwin's first full-size locomotive was built for the Philadelphia, Germantown and Norristown Railroad Company—a short-line horsedrawn railroad typical for its time. There was no local machinery, manpower or expertise extant for the production of steam locomotives when Baldwin began filling the PG&N's order; it all had to be done absolutely from scratch. Cylinders were bored with a chisel set in a wooden block—a crude 'jig' which had to be positioned by hand. Even the welding of the necessary iron bars had to be done as if for the first time; local blacksmiths had no expertise with materials that were thick enough.

Previous pages: The *John Bull* in passenger service. *At right:* Robert Stevens, president of the Camden & Amboy, was impressed by the British-built Stephenson locomotives. Stevens bought the Stephenson *John Bull,* which was based on the Stephenson *Planet* design— an advance on the first Stephenson product, *Rocket,* which is shown *below.*

On 23 November 1832, Baldwin's *Old Ironsides* was christened and ready for testing. In the PG&N's trials of the locomotive, various problems were encountered: the pump valves fed too little water to the boiler, and at one point, the drivers slipped on the axle and the locomotive sank between the rails. On a run from Philadelphia to Germantown, which line had an ascending grade of 32 feet per mile ending in a half-mile grade of 45 feet per mile, the engine had much difficulty pulling its load.

Baldwin's asking price had been $4000. The PG&N offered, and he grudgingly accepted, $3500. He swore that he would never again build a locomotive, but as we know, a certain fascination was at work—that gleam in his eye had assumed the form of a locomotive; Baldwin's name would one day be nearly synonymous with the word 'locomotive.'

On 17 December 1832, approximately 55 people boarded a horsedrawn train from Bordentown to South Amboy on the Camden & Amboy Railroad. On 24 January 1833, the C&A's first horsedrawn train of three cars hauled approximately 19,500 pounds of freight. On

a September day in 1833, *John Bull* became the first passenger steam engine on the Camden & Amboy line. While the West Point Foundry's *Stourbridge Lion* was the very first locomotive to run on American rails, *John Bull* was the first passenger hauling locomotive in regular service in the US.

The Camden & Amboy's Robert Stevens and Isaac Dripps were to make many mechanical contributions to the future of railroading as well. Whittling seemed to be the inventor's mode in those days; Sam Colt whittled the cylinder mechanism for his famous revolvers out of a chunk of wood, inspired by the design of a ship's wheel, while on an ocean voyage as a young seaman. Another sort of wheel inspired young Robert Stevens— the wheel of a rail car, and how to keep it on track, and how to keep that track in service year after year. Like Colt, Stevens whittled his model in wood, amid the meditative roll and pitch of the ocean's waves. The skinny iron rail that he designed would combine, with the pugnacious little five-ton locomotive that he brought across the waves with him, to set in motion still larger

Above: An illustration of Matthias Baldwin's first full-size locomotive, *Old Ironsides*, hauling passenger coaches. This loco's design was inspired by a close look at the Camden & Amboy's *John Bull*, which is shown *below*, as modified by the inventive Robert Stevens and Isaac Dripps— with 'shack' tender and two-wheel truck.

Baldwin's *Old Ironsides (below)* weighed five tons and was built from scratch; even the fabricating tools had to be devised. Baldwin went on to become the largest supplier of steam locomotives in North America, keeping the Pennsy and many other railroads—which also often designed and built their own—well supplied with motive power.

wheels—the wheels of industrial commerce, and would bring to bear on the northeastern United States the very incarnation of those forces; the great railways of the 19th and 20th centuries, and in particular, the road bearing that familiar keystone sign, the Pennsylvania Railroad.

John Stevens

On 13 March 1823, the Pennsylvania state legislature granted Colonel John Stevens a charter to build a railroad from Philadelphia to Columbia. Stevens' dream was to expand the railroad area available to him; with a charter in New Jersey for the Camden & Amboy (which was the very first railroad charter granted in the US), and now a charter in Pennsylvania, Stevens had the basis, on paper at least, from which to build east across New Jersey, and west across Pennsylvania—opening up the possibility of a railroad that stretched from New York to the Great Lakes.

Though Stevens had already sponsored surveys for the Pennsylvania segment, railroads were known by investors to be expensive affairs, really not much at an advantage over canals, which were a tried and true means of shipment—from an investor's eye view, even a well mapped-out railway was a risky venture. In short, investors balked at Stevens' ambitious enterprise. Canal syndicates were then powerful, and various politicians joined in the chorus *against* building railroads—and in favor of building canals.

A Canal to the West

Since no actual construction was being done, and Stevens seemed to be severely balked for the time being, the Pennsylvania state legislature set up a commission to study the feasibility of a canal route to the West.

This commission was formed in the nick of time—or so it must have seemed. Here was Philadelphia, queen city of commerce for the up and coming United States, and she was being threatened by her upstart sister to the east, New York. In 1825, the Erie Canal opened its path across New York State, effectively drawing all westward bound port business through New York City, and seriously diminishing Philadelphia's power as the shipping trade portal to the growing country.

Philadelphia merchants were alarmed, to say the least. The gentry of the town were up in arms, possessed by the same vision about which the merchants tossed in their beds: Philadelphia, demoted to second-class status by her loss in trade, and *all their profits* swept away by the mercantile waters of the Erie Canal.

In 1826, Pennsylvania passed an act commissioning the Pennsylvania Canal, which was meant to forge across the state to the Ohio River and its considerably lucrative trade arteries. That same year, an act repealing the Stevens charter granted railroading rights to the Columbia, Lancaster & Philadelphia Railroad Company, but the CL&P fared little better than had the Stevens' proposed line.

Ground was broken near Harrisburg for the Pennsylvania Canal on 4 July 1826. In 1827, the state directed the canal commission to prepare construction plans for a railroad to cover the same route as the CL&P—which had been commissioned to serve the same territory as Stevens' road.

The State Road

This state-commissioned road would run from Philadelphia to Columbia, at the Susquehanna River. A line from Huntingdon to Johnstown was also planned. A joint appropriation for these two railroads and the canal was made in the sum of $2 million. The entire network would come to be known as the State Road of Public Works; a chain of canals, railroads, motor-assisted 'incline planes' and one tunnel spanning the state and connecting Philadelphia to Pittsburgh—thereby creating the all-important trade corridor to the west which would draw trade once more into Philadelphia's port.

The line from Philadelphia to Columbia would, as is railroading custom, bear the names of its termini: it would be called the Philadelphia & Columbia Railroad. Major John Wilson layed the line out, and on 24 March 1828, the state authorized construction on the road, and two million dollars were set aside for the commencement of construction on 20 miles of roadbed at either end of the route, building in toward the center.

What began with Colonel John Stevens as a private enterprise had become a public trust. By the end of December 1829, 40 miles of grading had been completed, including viaducts and bridges. The line began at the corner of Broad and Vine Streets in Philadelphia and crossed the Schuylkill below Peter Island. On the west bank of the river was an inclined plane, called the Belmont Inclined Plane, which was used to haul cars up a half-mile seven percent grade to the high ground above the river. The line stayed on the level for several miles before descending into the Chester Valley to Lancaster, and thence to Columbia, where another inclined plane let the cars down to the canal basin by the Susquehanna, where the Pennsylvania Canal began. The 40 miles so far completed were used as feeder lines to supply materials for the road's ongoing construction. The road was finally completed, successfully negotiating the above-described route, on 20 September 1832.

The first locomotive to roll on the Philadelphia & Columbia was a Norris-built engine called the *Green Hawk*, which made a nine-hour round trip from Philadelphia to Paoli (and vice versa) in late 1832. Previous to this, of course, all P&C commerce had been horse drawn. The Commonwealth contracted Matthias Baldwin to build a second locomotive for the P&C (aka the 'State Road'). Baldwin's reputation as a locomotive builder had been growing since his earliest efforts at transportation designing. The locomotive he built for the State Road was patterned after the *Planet* class locos, and it had a four wheel bogie, or truck, added to its fore end to replace its carrying wheels.

Baldwin's loco for the State Road was called the *Lancaster*— this was joined by another Baldwin loco, of the same design, called the *Columbia*.

Lancaster and *Columbia* were fired up and ready to go when the P&C was officially opened on 7 October 1834. The trains they hauled carried a delegation of dignitaries including the state governor, the canal commissioners and other VIPs, including railroad personnel and guests. Leaving Columbia at 8 am, they arrived in Philadelphia at 6 pm.

Horses, however, were used in the prime force of the railroad until, upon examination of burdenage records, it was shown that *Lancaster* had hauled up to 19 fully burdened cars over the steepest and highest grades between Philadelphia and Columbia. This was an unprecedented performance, and spelled the beginning of the end for horses as the nation's prime movers. By 1836, locomotives had superseded horse cars— the Philadelphia & Columbia had over 17 locomotives in use by then.

The inclined planes in use on this road were equipped with a heavy rope, which was attached to the rail cars at the beginning of the grades. This rope then 'reeled in' by a 60 horse-power stationary engine situated at the top of the grade. In a similar manner, rope was let out at a

measured pace to lower cars down the grades when they were going in the opposite direction.

Besides being hazardous, this system was expensive to run— operating costs for the P&C were high, and the potential accident rate, let alone the accidents that had already occurred, compounded the State Road's worries, and alternate routes were planned.

One of these alternates, the West Philadelphia Railroad Company, was incorporated in 1835. Suffering the same economic woes that other early attempts at building railroads suffered, the WPRR was taken over by the Canal Commission while the road was still in construction. The road branched out from the P&C at Ardmore and ended at the Schuylkill just south of Philadelphia's Market Street. When the road was finished in 1850,

Above: This November 1896 photograph shows the Baldwin Locomotive Works in Philadelphia, as viewed from the corner of 17th Street and Pennsylvania Avenue. From this factory proceeded most of North America's steam locomotive power in the 19th and 20th centuries. Matthias Baldwin himself (inset) started out as a watchmaker, but became the single most important locomotive builder in the United States, whose business grew as the country—and its railroads—grew.

trains were routed over this line, and the Belmont inclined plane was abandoned.

An existing bridge across the Schuylkill was reinforced and modified to carry two railroad tracks, and in 1852 a passenger depot was built at 18th and Market Streets in Philadelphia. The old line east of this was leased to private enterprise, and in 1852, the Pennsylvania Railroad bought it, as it would so many small railroads in the years to follow.

The Middle Division Canal joined the Philadelphia & Columbia at Columbia, then followed the Susquehanna River's east shore to Middletown, where the canal merged with the river. At Duncan's Island, the canal separated from the river once more, and coursed along the Juniata River Valley as far as Hollidaysburg. It gave

way at Hollidaysburg to the Allegheny Portage Railroad, which was a complex line composed of 10 inclined planes, four viaducts, two sets of tracks and one 900-foot tunnel—the Staple Bend Tunnel, the first railroad tunnel in the United States.

Approved by the state legislature on 21 March 1831, the Allegheny Portage ran from Hollidaysburg up a series of five inclined planes to the top of Blair's Gap—a rise of 1398 feet in 10 miles. In the west side of the Al-

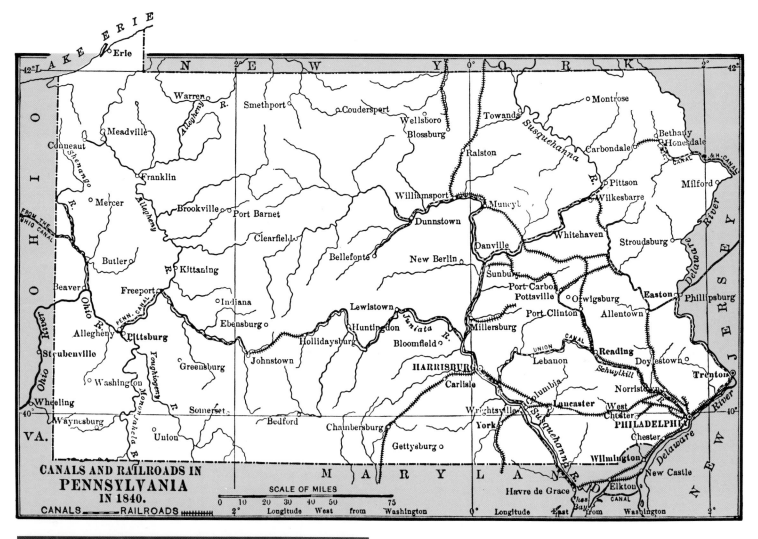

CANALS AND RAILROADS IN
PENNSYLVANIA
IN 1840.

CANALS ----- RAILROADS ++++++++

SCALE OF MILES

legheny Mountains, trains descended via another series of five inclined planes at the rate of 1172 feet in 20 miles. Two 30-horsepower engines were installed at the top of each incline. The engines were used alternately, to save wear and tear on them, and to assure that at least one engine would be operable in case of emergency. An ascending train and a descending train would make their respective transits at the same time, which insured balance, as both would be attached by the rope to the same engine. Braking on this plane system consisted of the brakes on the cars themselves, a power operated brake on the upper pulley wheel and a 'buck' or braking car, attached to the downhill end of the train.

In the level stretches between planes, horses— and later, locomotives— moved the cars. Each train left its engine at the start of a plane, and after its five-minute ascent or descent, it picked up another engine for the next level stretch.

From Johnstown, where the Allegheny Portage Railroad left off, the Western Division Canal followed the Conemaugh, Kiskiminetas and Allegheny river valleys through a system of 152 bridges, 16 aqueducts, 66 locks and a 1000-foot tunnel. This canal system rose 465 feet over its course, and occasional low water periods stimulated the building of a dam on the Conemaugh River— this same dam would fail in 1889, causing the catastrophic Johnstown Flood.

This Canal system made the final link to Pittsburgh, and while engineering marvels like the tunnels, inclined planes and canals were impressive, they were horribly expensive to build and operate, and they seemed to actually generate delays. Nearly $80 million had been spent in original construction costs for this state-owned

Colonel John Stevens *(opposite)* wanted to build a line from the Great Lakes to New York City via Philadelphia. The State Line of Public Works *(above left)*—a system of railroads and canals linking Pittsburgh to Philadelphia—was built on a route Stevens had planned to build. *Above:* A 4–4–0 woodburner, uncoupled from its train, makes a fuel stop while one of its crew chats with friends. *At right:* One of the first sophisticated dining cars. Note the lamps hung in the clerestory.

railroads-and-canals transport system, and an additional $40 million in debt accumulated over the years of the system's operation. It was finally bought by the Pennsylvania Railroad on 27 July 1857.

Between 1830 and 1835, more railroad building was done in Pennsylvania than in any other state. The urge to preserve Philadelphia's status as the merchant city of the United States resulted in some 200 miles of rails being opened during these years. The state system connected Philadelphia to Pittsburgh and the very important Ohio River transport routes.

The early years of railroad building in the United States gave seed to dozens of under-funded small railways; investor faith and legislative approval governed the growth of American railroads. But that new phenomenon, the steam locomotive, could make these rather cumbersome horse- and stationary engine-powered railways actually compete with and almost immediately supersede the tried and not always true canal system. This sense which sprang forth in the early 1830's would cause investors and legislatures to take an increasing interest in railroads, and railroads were soon to be emblematic of power, prestige and money.

Many of these roads were, though no one knew it at the time, forming a nucleus for what would become the world's largest railroad, a paragon of efficiency, luxury and engineering acumen: the Pennsylvania Railroad.

THE PENNSYLVANIA RAILROAD

Organization

On 6 March 1838, the merchants of Philadelphia and other concerned citizens approached Charles E Schlatter to survey routes for a possible alternative to the State Works System— as it was called— of railroads and canals. It had been seen that the State System was inadequate to the task of competing with New York's Erie Canal. Massive amounts of money were at stake, Philadelphia's prestige was on the line, and the general welfare of the Commonwealth of Pennsylvania stood to rise or fall according to the success or failure of establishing an efficient, cross-state transport system.

Schlatter finished his surveying in 1840 and reported on the existence of three possible routes, of which the interested parties chose one that followed the Juniata and Conemaugh valleys. The race was on: in 1845, the Baltimore & Ohio Railroad was petitioning to build a line into Pittsburgh, and in April of 1846, the B&O was granted permission to do so— if the whippersnapper railroad newly requested at a public meeting in 1845, and incorporated on 13 April 1846, could not fulfill the conditions of its charter. This 'upstart,' of course, was the Pennsylvania Railroad. With its incorporation capital of $10 million the Pennsy had to fulfill three conditions or the B&O would be given the opportunity to swallow up Pennsylvania's western trade routes. These conditions were that 30 miles of actual road bed were to be under contract, $3 million in investor subscriptions to the railroad were to be 'firmed up' and at least $1 million was to actually have been brought into its treasury by 30 July 1847. By July 1847, the monetary obligations of the charter were fulfilled, and on that very date, the first 20 miles west of Harrisburg were let under contract, and 15 miles east of Pittsburgh were also contracted. The B&O's rights were voided in August of that year.

First President

The Pennsy's organizational form had actually been set up on 30 March 1847. Thirteen directors were duly elected, and among them were Samuel V Merrick and William C Patterson, the men who would be the Pennsy's first two presidents.

Merrick's election the very next day was a foregone conclusion, as he had been one of the most vociferous supporters of the railroad. Civic minded, Merrick was one of the founders of the Franklin Institute, and served as its president from 1842 to 1854.

Merrick left the railroad in 1849, as he and his business partner, John Henry Towne, had built the Southwark Iron Foundry and the Philadelphia Gas Works, and these two businesses were growing by leaps and bounds.

As is mentioned elsewhere in this text, John Edgar Thompson was appointed chief engineer for the building of the new line, and assisting him were Edward Miller and William B Foster. It is a significant fact that Miller and Foster were originally intended to confer directly with the board of directors. But this, which was Merrick's edict, was simply ignored by Thomson, who declared that his associates should be responsible to himself.

Both Merrick and his successor came up against this attitude. The Pennsy stockholders and many of its personnel simply placed no value on the presidency unless the president was a true-blue engineer, a builder who knew the whys and wherefores of railroad construction.

If one can speak in such a manner about corporate bodies, this was the 'spirit' of the Pennsy speaking up, for, as late as the 1920s, Pennsy policy was to educate its officers from the ground up: an institutionalized 'working your way to the top,' and the grounding these men received in solid railroading paid historically large dividends in terms of the Pennsy's many successes.

WC Patterson was elected on 1 September 1849. Under him, the same leadership qualities which were evident in the Merrick regime shown forth in Chief Engineer John Edgar Thomson, who lobbied fearlessly for the spectacular new construction which had to be done on the Pennsy's mountainous route. Push west, push west against competition from New York and Maryland, which competition would continue as a Pennsy theme for many years.

Patterson left office on 2 February 1852. Stepping into his place, and achieving a great many of the acquisitions which would bring the Pennsy to its basic working contours, was Thomson, who was the first of five Pennsy presidents in what would be viewed later as the Pennsy's glory days.

The Pennsy Commences

The Pennsy opened its first track section on 1 September 1849, and this provided a rail link from Harrisburg to Lewistown. By September 1850, the tracks had reached Mountain House and the last mile from there to

Previous pages: A Currier & Ives countryside, with early passenger train. The first presidents of the Pennsylvania Railroad: An early proponent of the Pennsy, civic-minded Samuel V Merrick *(above left)* served from 31 March 1847 to 1 September 1849; William C Patterson *(above)* served from 1 September 1849 to 2 February 1852. J Edgar Thomson, the Pennsy's chief engineer, became president following Patterson; Thomson both built and organized the Pennsy's foundation.

Hollidaysburg was soon completed, allowing the Pennsy to link up with the Allegheny Portage Railroad on 1 October 1850.

The western end of the line was completed by 10 December 1852, when the first through train made its run from Philadelphia to Pittsburgh. This train started its journey on the Philadelphia & Columbia Railroad, continued on the Pennsy and barreled into Pittsburgh on the rails of the Allegheny Portage.

The Pennsy built its first station at 11th and Market Streets in Philadelphia and opened it for business on 20 May 1854. The new railroad had made an agreement with the Philadelphia & Columbia on 20 May 1854.

As chief engineer of the railroad J Edgar Thomson had, previous to this, built the Georgia Railroad. Under his capable guidance, the Pennsy had become operational. Now, on 15 February 1854, the line would complete its own tracks into Philadelphia, and the possibility of riding from Philadelphia to Pittsburgh on one railroad was rapidly becoming a reality.

The trip took from 13 to 17 hours, and initially, three trains per day made the run. The State Works System was now mere competition—it was also a tremendous burden to the Commonwealth, as due to mismanagement and the fact that its canal segments froze solid in winter, halting its operations, the system was rolling up terrible debts. The state offered it for sale on 24 April 1854, but at the asking price of $20 million, no one was

buying. In 1855, the price was dropped to $10 million and there were still no takers.

On 16 May 1857, the State Works System again 'went on the block.' At $7.5 million the price was right. An additional sweetner in the form of a stipulation was added thusly: if the Pennsylvania Railroad, yes the Pennsy, were the purchaser, for a mere $1.5 million extra, it would never again have to pay the Commonwealth the kind of freight tonnage taxes that were at the time regularly levied against transport companies in Pennsylvania.

The Pennsy bought the State Works on 27 June 1857, and used the New Portage Railroad's tracks over the Alleghenies until its own through line was completed. The New Portage had been built to eliminate the problems inherent in the Allegheny Portage's inclined planes; therefore, when the New Portage opened for business in 1855, sans inclined planes, the Allegheny Portage was abandoned.

On 18 July 1858, the first Pennsylvania Railroad train rode Pennsylvania Railroad tracks all the way from Philadelphia to Pittsburgh.

The year 1850 marked the rapid merging of many of the early, small railroads into longer roads under one management. The United States was expanding, its population was increasing; with faster machines, and stiffer competition, the public imperative became the demand for speed and ready access; delivery of goods had to be reliable, as city merchants with one eye on their competitors and one eye on their customers' wants insisted that they needed their goods as soon as possible. The day of the small railroad was numbered. The day of the consolidation, the merger and the buyout was here.

Probably the first privately built railroad acquired by the Pennsy was the Harrisburg, Portsmouth, Mt Joy & Lancaster Railroad, chartered in 1832 and whose first president was James Buchanan. On 1 November 1848, the Pennsy leased this road for 20 years. Its route from Harrisburg to Dillersville (connecting with the Philadelphia & Columbia) would come in handy, the (yet-to-be-completed) Pennsy's management thought. This 20 year lease was later extended to 999 years—long enough, one would think.

J Edgar Thomson

Under J Edgar Thomson's guiding hand the basic body of the Pennsy system took shape. In the following pages, some of the earliest roads which were taken into the Pennsy to comprise this nucleus are treated from a historical perspective. This is, of course, an overview. By its 100th anniversary, the Pennsy comprised properties formerly owned by more than 200 companies.

The Camden & Amboy Railroad

In 1815, the New Jersey Legislature gave John Stevens the first railroad charter in the United States, authorizing him to 'erect a railroad from the River Delaware near Trenton to the Raritan at or near New Brunswick.' Stevens couldn't raise the funds for the venture, but in 1830 the state of New Jersey gave Stevens another chance, with a catch.

The proponents of a canal between the Delaware and the Raritan Rivers had been lobbying long and hard, so the New Jersey Legislature granted charters to Stevens' railroad, to be called the Camden & Perth Amboy Railroad, and to his canal-going competitors, the Delaware & Raritan Canal Company.

On 15 February 1831, the two companies combined their stock, but elected separate officers and directors, and thereby became the 'twin companies,' officially known as the Camden & Amboy Railroad & Delaware & Raritan Canal Companies. Stevens' son Robert was named president of the Camden & Amboy Railroad and his son Edwin was named treasurer.

The digging commenced for the Delaware & Raritan Canal in 1831. Finally, the entirety of the Delaware & Raritan Canal, with its 14 110-foot by 24-foot locks, was put into operation in 1838.

The Camden & Amboy also began its construction in 1831, and by 1834 the 61 miles from Perth Amboy to Camden was finished and a locomotive successfully ran the distance. In 17 December 1832, the road's first passengers were taken from Bordentown to South Amboy via horsecars. On 24 January 1833, the line's first freight—three cars with approximately 7000 pounds burdenage each—was horsedrawn. In September of 1833, the *John Bull* pulled its first train, from Bordentown to South Amboy.

The line to Camden was opened in 1834 and the rail route via the Philadelphia & Trenton railroad was opened in 1834. There was much protest against the perceived transportation monopoly that the Camden & Amboy & Delaware & Raritan Canal Companies had in the state of New Jersey. Their main competition was the New Jersey Railroad, chartered 7 March 1832 and operable from the Hudson River to Elizabeth in 1834. The New Jersey pushed its line from Elizabeth to New Brunswick in 1835–36.

The Camden & Amboy's directors sought to 'head the opposition off at the pass.' They bought up a controlling interest in both the Trenton Bridge Company and in the Philadelphia & Trenton Railroad.

Despite keen competitive natures, both the Camden & Amboy's and the New Jersey Railroad's directors saw that an all-rail route from Philadelphia to New York would be of mutual advantage. Besides, one could 'one-up' the competition that much better when the stakes were higher.

In September of 1836, the Camden & Amboy made an agreement with the New Jersey Railroad to build a connecting line from New Brunswick to Bordentown, thus spanning the state with a rail route composed of their two companies. The financial panic of 1837 delayed work on this link route until June of 1838. The route was completed just after the new year.

In the 1860s the New Jersey became unhappy with its agreement with the Camden & Amboy. Seeking advantage, the New Jersey projected a parallel line to Trenton, and the Camden & Amboy countered with a proposed line to Hoboken. Negotiations began in 1865 and the Camden & Amboy merged with the New Jersey Railroad in 1867. The two railways became the United New Jersey Railways & Canal Company.

This independent union continued until 1 July 1871 when, under the terms of a 999-year lease, the United

New Jersey became part of the Pennsylvania Railroad system. The formal transfer of the line to the Pennsy was completed on 1 December 1871.

Locomotives used on the Camden & Amboy are traceable from the *John Bull*, a tender for which was created from a four wheel flat car fitted with a whiskey cask which fed its water to the engine's boiler via a shoe leather hose.

The *John Bull* was fine for straight stretches, but got ornery on curves, causing much excitement among its crew; it tended to jump the track. Robert Stevens and Isaac Dripps devised a four-wheel 'truck,' which swivelled on a pivot and fit under the front of the locomotive. This was one of the first such devices used in American railroading and it greatly enhanced the *John Bull's* agility on curves, as it served to stabilize the locomotive by 'steering' it.

Stevens made another trip to England in 1848 and was duly impressed by the fast, large-drivered British Crampton engines. Cramptons had a single pair of drivers, and seemed easily copiable. Stevens returned to the US and asked Isaac Dripps to design an American Crampton with eight-foot drivers. The result, built by Richard Norris & Son in November 1848, was slow to get started, but very fast once under way. Stevens became disaffected with the design's low tractive force—

Above: This illustration shows the *John Bull* pulling a string of early passenger cars for the Camden & Amboy. This engine was the first passenger locomotive in regular use in the US. Note the design variations between this depiction and those on pages 10–11 and 14–15.

five to six cars were its limit in hauling capacity— and opted for designs with more torque capacity. He was overruled, and several more of these American Cramptons, of varying wheel size, went to work for Steven's railroad, and served until 1862. One of their number, revamped as a 4–4–0, rode the rails until 1865.

Robert Stevens and Isaac Dripps designed and built what may have been an attempt at an early 'heavy freight' locomotive— the *Monster.* The appropriately named 30-ton *Monster* may have been the first eight-wheel connected engine in the United States. Although the wheel arrangement was 0–8–0, it was not a true 0–8–0 since spur gears, rather than connecting rods, were used to couple the second and third driving axles. Four locomotives based on the *Monster* design were built in 1852 and 1854 by the Trenton Locomotive Works, of which Dripps was a partner, for the Camden & Amboy Railroad.

The Northern Central Railway

It has been said that the decade of the 1850s was one of the most important chapters in the annals of railroad history. Due to the increase in industrialization in the northeastern United States, the continued western expansion of the new country and the abundant natural resources of the Great Lakes region, railroads had become important as cargo and passenger transport systems. Now it was time to make them optimally effective and lucrative. Owners of short-line roads realized that greater profits could be made if they could consolidate regionally with former competitors. There was money to be had in westward expansion and in serving the increasingly healthy industry of the young United States of America.

The Northern Central was incorporated in the 1850s. One of the roads it comprised was the Baltimore & Susquehana, which was one of the first railroads in the US, having been chartered on 13 February 1828. Seven miles of the road were finished from the fall of 1830, when its actual construction commenced, to 7 August 1832, when the *Herald,* a *Planet*-class Stephenson locomotive, made its first trip on the line. The little British loco was a success and the Baltimore & Susquehanna was stretched its full length to York, Pennsylvania in 1838.

The Northern Central effectively was a consolidation of the Baltimore & Maryland, the York & Cumberland, the York & Maryland and the Susquehanna Railroads. In 1858, connection with the Pennsylvania Railroad was made at Marysville via a 128-mile branch line from Baltimore, Maryland to Sunbury, Pennsylvania.

The Baltimore & Ohio Railroad acquired a majority of the Northern Central's stock, but the Northern Central was in bad financial straights and its holdings went on the block in 1861. The Pennsylvania Railroad bought more than 43,000 shares in the company. Previous to this, officers of the Pennsy had acquired Northern Central shares in London, and together with the 1861 purchase, these shares now amounted to a majority ownership in the Northern Central.

By 1866, the Northern Central comprised 326 miles of trackage by way of its operational control of the Wrightsville, York & Gettysburg, connecting York with Wrightsville; the Shamokin Valley & Pottsville, connecting Sunbury with Elmira; the Chemung Road, connecting Elmira to Watkins Glen; and the Jefferson & Canandaigua, connecting Watkins Glen to Canandaigua.

The Northern Central/Pennsy now had connections to Baltimore, but the B&O, which had trackage from Baltimore to Washington, DC, refused to provide through service in any form for any entity of the Pennsy road. Therefore, the Baltimore & Potomac was proposed as an alternate means to connect with the nation's capitol.

But opposition to such a through line in direct competition to the B&O was strong, and the line's charter finally approved a 73-mile main line to Pope's Creek, which would be allowed branches of no more than 20 miles in length.

As of July 1873, branch upon branch had been built with the final leg to Washington (extending from Bowie, Maryland) going into operation on the aforementioned date. A tunnel was built at Baltimore in 1873 and the Pennsy had access—via the Northern Central and its operating companies—to the nation's capital.

The Philadelphia & Erie Railroad

Yet another short line with financial woes, the P&E was incorporated on 3 April 1837, having a capital of $3 million.

Unfortunately, the Bank of the United States collapsed in 1837–38, and extensions to the railroad's charter deadline had to be gotten. Extensions to 1840, then 1851, 1858 and 1860 were successively granted.

The City of Philadelphia subscribed $2 million in 1854, on the basis of actual work completed to that time. The line forged on to Williamsport that same year, and the first train ran into Sunbury on 10 January 1856. By 1860, over 200 miles of roadbed had been prepared, bridges laid in, etc; over 100 miles of track had been actually put down. But that year saw the road with a general lack of funds, and work was halted.

The road had begun life under the moniker of the Sunbury & Erie Railroad, but in March 1861 the state of Pennsylvania changed the line's name to the Philadelphia & Erie, perhaps hoping that the charm of the name would help matters.

At any rate, if completed the little road would provide a handy transportation route from northern central to northwest Pennsylvania; access from the heartland to the Great Lakes, so to speak. The Pennsylvania Railroad, ever opportunistic, advanced the money to complete the road in its 287 and one-half mile totality, under the terms of a 999-year lease.

In 1864, the line from Sunbury to the Great Lakes was completed, and Pennsy had added yet more useable roadbed to its increasing bulk.

The Pittsburgh, Fort Wayne & Chicago Railroad

The PFW&C was a consolidation of three separate roads that had been built as westward-heading lines stretching from the western border of Pennsylvania. These lines were the Ohio & Pennsylvania Railroad, the Ohio & Indiana Railroad and the Fort Wayne & Chicago Railroad.

The story of these roads illustrates the basic shrewdness of the Pennsylvania Railroad management.

The Ohio & Pennsylvania was chartered in 1848 to build from Mansfield, Ohio to Columbiana County and thence to Pittsburgh, Pennsylvania. A western Ohio extension was to reach from Mansfield to the western border of Ohio. It would make a wonderful beginning for any railroad looking to feed its operations from the huge markets of the rapidly growing Midwest. The Pennsy bought $300,000 in capital stock of the O&P in 1852. Upon completion of its 187 miles of trackage in 1853, the Pennsy looked forward to helping with the financial well-being of a proposed adjoining line to this railroad—the Ohio & Indiana. This was another $300,000 capital stock purchase which was made upon completion of substantial construction. Construction commenced in 1852 and its route from Crestline, Ohio to Fort Wayne, Indiana, was complete in November of 1854.

Incorporated in 1852, the Fort Wayne & Chicago Railroad Company ran into funding problems and the Pennsylvania abstained from stock purchasing on this line (construction had hardly begun as late as 1856). In August of 1856 the lines mentioned in this section merged with the beleaguered FW&CR and became the Pittsburgh, Fort Wayne & Chicago Railroad.

The Pennsylvania couldn't resist, and assisted the completion of this line through to Chicago. Rebellion was in the works though, and despite the Pennsy's help and its expectations that the PFW&C would loyally serve as its through line to Chicago, PFW&C directors tried to lay independent tracks to the east—thus competing with the Pennsy. The line was foolish in this, for it was not doing well financially. Jay Gould and his cronies nearly scooped it up, but fast thinking by Pennsy officials resulted in a 7 June 1869 lease for 999 years, eagerly granted by the now bedraggled PFW&C management—the Gould stock buyout attempt was a harrowing experience.

The Philadelphia, Baltimore & Washington RR Company

Both the Philadelphia & Delaware County Railroad and the Southward Railroad were chartered on 2 April 1831. Pennsylvanians felt that access to ports on Delaware Bay and other points south certainly would feed freight business destined for the greater continental US through Philadelphia.

Above: The Chicago Railroad Fair in 1948 saw this reproduction of an early locomotive based on the *John Bull/Planet* design. These quirky little five-ton locomotives proved the worth of rail steam power.

The year 1832 saw the chartering of the Wilmington & Susquehanna, the Delaware & Maryland and the Baltimore & Port Deposit.

On 14 July 1837, this line of connecting roads was opened between Baltimore and Philadelphia. Early in 1838, all of the above mentioned roads were consolidated into the Philadelphia, Wilmington & Baltimore Railroad. In 1881, upon buying a majority in PW&B stock, the Pennsylvania Railroad managed to snatch the PW&B out from under the B&O Railroad's avaricious nose.

In November 1902, the PW&B and the Baltimore & Potomac (see the Northern Central Railroad discussed previously) were merged to become the Philadelphia, Baltimore & Washington Railroad Company.

The Long Island Railroad

This road was fated to be a steppingstone for one of the Pennsylvania's finest achievements— the building of Pennsylvania Station in New York City and its six feeder tunnels under the North River and the Hudson.

Incorporated on 24 April 1834, the Long Island Railroad was to run from Brooklyn to Greenport; there it would connect with a ferry line across Long Island Sound to Connecticut, where the New York, Providence & Boston Railroad further progressed.

This typical-for-the-time hybrid water and rail route satisfied a popular desire for a New York to Boston freight and passenger line. The Long Island leased the Brooklyn & Jamaica Railroad, thereby saving itself some construction cost. Beginning construction in April of 1836 was therefore commenced eastward from Jamaica, New York. On 1 March 1837, a section from Jamaica to Hicksville opened. The panic of 1837 delayed the line's completion to Greenport until 29 July 1844.

The outstanding reason that the Long Island was built— to provide the first leg of such a roundabout route to Boston— was that a more direct attack was considered to be impossible, due to the lay of the land along such a hypothetically more direct route. Travel time from New York to Boston along the LI-ferry-NYP&B was 10 hours one way at optimum.

A direct route to Boston was established in 1848, due to improvements in railroading techniques and equipment, and by 1850 the LI became a local carrier. In the 1870s rival lines were built on either side of the LI, and by the early 1890s these three lines, which were choking one another by dint of their close quarters competition, chose the better part of corporate valor and merged.

The Pennsy acquired a majority of the Long Island's stock in 1900.

The West Jersey & Seashore Railroad

On 5 February 1853 the West Jersey Railroad was chartered, and opened from Camden to Bridgeton on 25 July 1861.

The Millville & Glassboro Railroad was chartered 9 March 1859, and opened in 1862. On 18 March 1868, the New Jersey state legislature approved the combination of the M&G with the WJ under the name of the West Jersey Railroad Company.

On 9 March 1863, the Cape May & Millville Railroad was chartered. Having opened in fall of that same year, the CM&M operated independently until 1868 when the West Jersey leased the CM&M.

In 1896 the West Jersey & Seashore was formed by a consolidation of these lines—which had been acquired by the Pennsy by lease of the United Railroads of New Jersey in 1871—with a line from Newfield to Atlantic City, the West Jersey & Atlantic Railroad, which had been chartered in 1879, and opened in mid-1880.

Running parallel to the lines discussed above, the Atlantic City Railroad had been built as a narrow gauge line. The Atlantic City went bankrupt and was acquired by the Reading Railroad in 1883. The Reading rebuilt this route for standard gauge and double tracks and thus went into direct competition with the Pennsy system for southern New Jersey freight and passenger business. The Camden & Atlantic, another Pennsy acquisition via the United Railroads of New Jersey deal, was by this time a part of the West Jersey & Seashore complex, and it was a direct route from Camden to Atlantic City. Thus, the Reading was competing with its double track line against two Pennsy lines.

The business that was the subject of this competition was seasonal: most of it was summer trade going into and out of Atlantic City. In the 1920's, both trunk lines saw that they were losing business to the highways, to each other and to the seasons themselves. Consolidation of these parallel lines was in order.

An agreement was reached in 1932 whereby the Pennsy bought the majority of the Atlantic City's stock for one dollar per share, and assigned its lease of the West Jersey & Seashore to the Atlantic City. Effective on 15 July 1933, the Atlantic City Railroad was renamed the Pennsylvania-Reading Seashore Lines.

Thus the foundations for the Pennsy empire were laid with these roads, and literally hundreds of smaller acquisitions made in the 1860s and 1870s, under the guiding hands of Pennsy presidents John Edgar Thomson, Alexander Scott, and their successors.

The big-drivered British Crampton locos were very fast for their time. Robert Stevens and Isaac Dripps attempted to build an American Crampton *(right)*; this type of engine had poor weight distribution and very weak traction, which ultimately led to the development of the famed 4–4–0 American design, a happy blend of speed *and* traction.

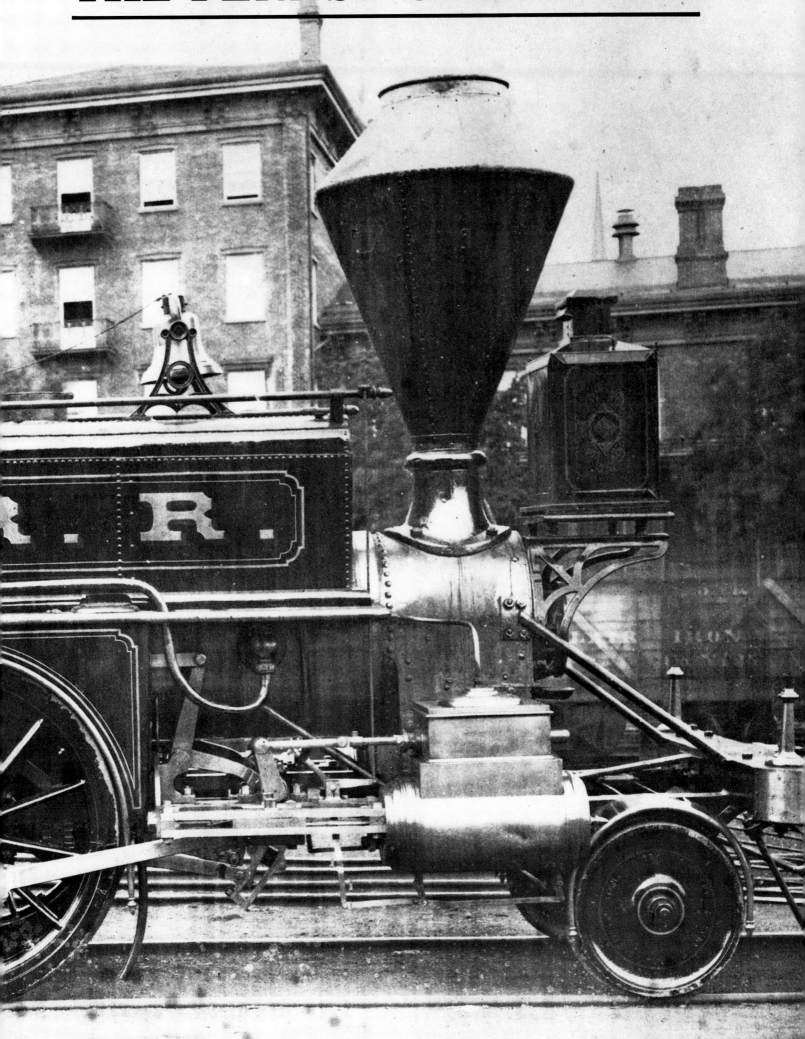

The Civil War

The Main Line of Public Works, that gangling amalgamation of canals and railroad tracks, had been bought by the Pennsylvania Railroad. There was a war on, yet north of the Mason-Dixon Line, there was a war within a war. Railroads were being built to an unprecedented degree; they were needed, as men and supplies had to be moved, and moved swiftly.

Under Pennsy president J Edgar Thomson, the old Main Line from Philadelphia to Pittsburgh was being replaced with 236 miles of railroad which ran through tunnels and over bridges, and had improved gradients and other engineering feats made possible by Thomson's engineering knowledge, gained in visiting European rail facilities.

Thomson, together with engineering genius Herman Haupt, had laid down the original Pennsy line, including the spectacular Horseshoe Curve which, starting just west of Altoona, rose over a 1.8 percent grade, to gain 122 feet from one horn of the curve to the other. It describes an arc doubling back over the Kittanning Valley.

Thomson was a cautious man in public—a reticent man who planned solidly and built his railroad with the utmost efficiency in mind. His second in command, Thomas A Scott, was more of the expansive school of thought: advantage, growth and profit were his motivators.

Herman Haupt had discovered young Scott while the latter was an agent for Leech and Company. While rising through the Pennsy ranks, Scott hired a young Scotsman, Andrew Carnegie, as a telegrapher. When he became vice president, Scott championed the cause of keeping the B&O out of Pittsburgh—a course of action that, while seeming advantagious to the Pennsy, was to make the Pittsburgh merchants angry at the railroad's monopoly on freight rates.

In 1861, a young surveyor named Alexander Cassatt was hired as a rodman in the engineering corps of the Pennsylvania Railroad. Thomson had an affinity for this young man's intelligence and refinement. They shared European travelling backgrounds and interests.

The talents of Haupt and Scott were soon called upon to aid their country. Scott had begun his career as a station agent in a tiny hamlet—the sort of place one would have called, even in the very rural Pennsylvania of the time, 'the sticks.' Within 10 years he'd risen to the vice-presidency of the road.

As of the outbreak of the Civil War, Scott was recognized as the finest operating executive in the nation. At President Lincoln's request, Governor Curtin of Pennsylvania borrowed Scott from the Pennsy. Scott's job was to move troops to the battle front as quickly and in as large a force as possible. He did his job supremely well, and when Confederate forces burned the Northern Central Railroad's bridges, Lincoln called upon Scott to repair the damage, making him a colonel in the US Army to grant him military authority with which to insure the cooperation of the personnel with whom he'd be working.

He finished the job ahead of time, returning to Washington to report to the President. The Northern Central was the swiftest route by which to reinforce troops in the nation's capital, which was hourly under threat of attack by the ever-strenghthening forces of the Confederacy.

Lincoln asked Scott eagerly, 'How is the road progressing, Colonel?'

'The road is completed,' Scott replied.

'Completed!' exclaimed Lincoln. 'How soon may we expect it to be open for troops?'

Scott answered, 'One train is already here with a regiment, and other trains are on the way.'

'Thank God!' Lincoln cried. 'Then we are all right again. There will be fewer sleepless eyes in Washington tonight.'

Scott was made Assistant Secretary of War and was given command of all government railroad activity. In that capacity, among other feats of railroadmanship, Scott rescued General Hooker, boxed in on Lookout Mountain in Tennessee by Confederate troops. Scott scoured six northern states for reinforcements, and assembled infantry, cavalry and field artillery regiments. These he hurried via rail to Hooker's aid, and the Union won the battle of Lookout Mountain on 24 November 1863, enabling General Ulysses S Grant to take Missionary Ridge on 25 November, which effectively delivered Chattanooga into the North's power.

Scott also instituted the wartime practice of protecting the President from possible assassination attempts by providing a decoy train or coach to lure would-be malefactors away from President Lincoln's actual travel route.

Herman Haupt, renowned for his construction and engineering work on the Pennsy, was also called away from the company to supervise railroad construction for the Union, and was made a general for his outstanding efforts.

At the end of the Civil War, railroads had become the mode of shipping goods. America's most prosperous canal, the Erie Canal, began the war carrying 2.25 million tons of freight for the year 1860. That same year, the Erie and the New York Central railroads moved approximately a million tons each. By 1865, the Erie and the New York Central moved about nine million tons of haulage, while the Erie Canal had moved three million tons. Railroads had taken over, for canals—while being cheaper—were slower, and in winter were unuseable due to freezing.

Alexander Cassatt

Young Cassatt rose through the ranks. In 1864 he was assigned the job of resident engineer for the middle division of the Philadelphia & Erie, which terminated on the west branch of the Susquehanna.

This road linked Pennsylvania's coal fields with East Coast markets, and in itself, Cassatt's engineering position was one of high responsibility. Yet his rise continued and the Pennsylvania Railroad's fortunes seemed to be 'going through the roof'; the increase in the anthracite coal industry during the Civil War was staggering. Pennsylvania coal fields were very rich in anthracite, and coal was the 'name of the game' for fast growth and profit. The Pennsy's revenues rose accordingly—$5 million in 1860 to $19.5 million in 1865.

Previous pages: Baldwin's 1000th locomotive, a 2–4–0 built for the Pennsy. *Below:* J Edgar Thomson, whose term in office included the Civil War and the great industrial expansion of the Northeast. *Above:* A Union Army 4–4–0 and tender bearing the name of Herman Haupt, who was borrowed from the Pennsy and made a general to build Union rails.

Steel and oil were soon to join coal as the breadwinners for the Pennsy, and the Pennsy would also literally roll on steel. The first steel rails ever rolled on order came from the Cambria Iron Works in Johnstown in 1867, and the main customer for these rails was Thomson's Pennsy.

The Erie and the B&O

Militating for a share, if not an outright takeover, of the Pennsy's freight-rich fields of operation were the B&O, which had temporarily taken a detour in its march northeast and been routed to Wheeling, and the Erie, a 500 mile long trunk line connecting New York harbor and the Great Lakes. The Erie was potentially a powerful competitor, but its strength was steadily drained by the neglect shown to its equipment, and its stock had been diluted to ridiculous extremes by its unscrupulous and speculative management.

Specifically, the Erie's management consisted of Daniel Drew, Jim Fisk and Jay Gould. They were to fight an intense and very costly war for control of the Erie with Cornelius Vanderbilt. Vanderbilt went on to buy a majority of stock in the New York Central, which would become the Pennsy's largest competitor.

By 1869, the Pennsy had extended its rails into the West, and among the lines the Pennsy gained control of was the Sunbury & Erie, renamed the Philadelphia & Erie. Returned from the war, Thomas Scott appeared in the P&E offices in Williamsport, where Alexander Cassatt had been recently assigned as Superintendent of Motive Power and Equipment.

Above: The Pennsy provided President Lincoln's funeral train— shown here is the engine and tender in their formal decorations at Baltimore, and behind them, the cars of the train, including the Pullman Silver Palace Sleeping Car *Pioneer*— see the text, page 62.

Scott wanted to check accounting figures and, instead of sending for a clerk who would bring the ledgers, Cassatt easily recalled the requested figures from memory.

The P&E had been losing over $250,000 per year. In Cassatt's first year as superintendent, he increased his 90 locomotives' rail mileage by 400,000 miles for the year, and decreased operating costs per mile by seven cents.

In his annual report to the P&E's stockholders in January 1867, Cassatt said, ' The expense of car repairs at this point has been largely increased by this want of adequate facilities. I would therefore respectfully urge on your consideration the importance of erecting car and paint shops during the present year.' He was granted his request.

Altoona

Cassatt's new station, Altoona, was a bustling, muddy village of 8000, clustered around the railroad's shops. Approaches to the town were of pristine Pennsylvania mountain beauty— the mountainsides woolly with trees, a landscape interrupted by small patches of cultivated land and clear mountain streams.

Altoona— a word derived from the Native American word 'allatoona,' meaning 'high lands of great worth'— was chosen in the 1840s when it was seen that increasing traffic would demand a better means of ascending and descending the Alleghenies than the old Portage Road's marvelous but inefficient inclined planes. J

Edgar Thomson had laid the place out on a tract of land bought by the railroad from an early settler named David Robeson for $11,000.

Locomotives ran from the newly established Altoona to Pittsburgh over the spectacular Horseshoe Curve. Originally only two tracks, the line grew under Cassatt's direction to four tracks, winding upward past Allegrippus, through the twin tunnels, reaching the summit at Gallitzin, having risen 1015 feet in the 11 mile distance from Altoona.

Amid the general industrial malaise of the town itself, the Pennsy tried to assert a note of elegance by building the luxury hotel, Logan House— reputed to serve the best ice cream in all the land. The hotel's plush red velvet interior— red velvet was *de riguer* for luxurious accomodations in those days— was framed by black walnut sashes and doorways, and large mirrors graced the walls. The town also had 12 churches and an opera house.

Cassatt soon proved himself. In November of 1867, Alexander Cassatt was appointed Superintendent of Machinery and Motive Power for the entire Pennsylvania Railroad.

Cassatt had tried to marry a minister's daughter— Harriet Buchanan, the niece of James Buchanan, who had been the President of the United States just previous to Abraham Lincoln. She rebuffed him. Curiously, or not curiously— as Alexander's sister was the soon-to-be renowned painter Mary Cassatt and there surely was some artistic abandon in his own psyche— Cassatt fell head over heels for Harriet's younger sister Lois! On 25 November 1868, Alexander Cassatt married Lois Buchanan, and brought her to their new home in Altoona. He had his wife; she had her important husband.

Cassatt was to prove himself to be of tremendous value to the Pennsy in the years to come.

Among other things, he stressed the standardization of locomotives to save repair and maintenance time, and the first eight classes of these standardized locomotives saw service between 1868 and 1872.

Also, as the Pennsy absorbed many smaller rail lines, the need for standardization of road widths became apparent. This, too, Cassatt implemented, making the entire Pennsy system a uniform track width of 4 feet 9 inches. The year was 1869 and Cassatt was named to the post of General Superintendent of the line.

Thomson created the position of General Manager for Cassatt, as he was pleased with Cassatt's handling of the leasing of the United Railroads of New Jersey. Cassatt's new office was at the Pennsylvania Railroad headquarters in Philadelphia. The Cassatts moved to Haverford, on the main line of the railroad, and were followed by many railroad executives and other wealthy men and their families, all of them interested in a country lifestyle which also afforded easy access to their offices in the city. Were these, perhaps, the first commuters?

The Pittsburgh Riots

On 27 May 1874, J Edgar Thomson died of a heart attack—the strains of bringing the Pennsy through the Panic of 1873 had made his already bad health worse. The Panic of 1873 was brought on when Congress investigated the financial underpinnings of Credit Mobilier—a scheme set up by several Union Pacific railroadmen to finance construction, charging outrageous fees, and giving the inflated profit to themselves and certain investors.

When the seamy underbelly of this kickback scam came to light, railroad stocks fell, businesses of all sorts were forced into receivership and thousands of workers lost their jobs.

A rate war on passenger and freight traffic was raging as railroads sought to recoup losses due to the Panic. Scott declared, 'During the first six months of 1877, not a farthing was made on through competitive freight by any line.' It was agreed, generally, that rail lines in the eastern US would unilaterally adjust their rates; and that the 10 percent reduction in wages—from executives to the lowest shop apprentices—would take effect on 1 July 1877. This reduction was the second such reduction in wages suffered by rail workers, the first having been made at the outset of the Panic, in 1873.

Trouble on the Lines

The first signs of trouble occurred on the B&O. The B&O's president insisted, despite wage cuts, on paying his stockholders a 10 percent dividend. This was considered an insult by B&O workers. On 17 July, B&O firemen blockaded the line at Martinsburg, West Virginia. The strike spread elsewhere. At Camden Junction, units of the Maryland militia, under orders to disperse the strikers there, were surrounded by stone-throwing mobs, and much violence occurred.

The wage reduction had been reluctantly accepted by Pennsy personnel, but another executive decision—which was attributed to Scott, who denied culpability—was made to doublehead all freights between Pittsburgh and Altoona. On the morning of the 19th, the brakemen and the fireman of the 8:40 refused to embark from Pittsburgh.

The dispatcher rounded up replacements, but the strikers had already persuaded other workers to join them, and armed with coupling pins, would not let the train depart. Incoming crews proved sympathetic and soon the Pittsburgh yards were locked down. Workers' families joined them, and local merchants, angry at what they felt was a Pennsy monopoly on Pittsburgh trade, proved sympathetic as well. Passenger trains were allowed to run; freight was immobile.

The mayor and the police refused to act. Alexander Cassatt, having risen to the post of third vice president in 1874, when Scott stepped into the presidency, assumed that the strike had ended when replacements had been found for the original striking Pennsy crew. He hadn't heard of the ensuing disorder until the next day, and when he heard about it, there was still more news: deputy superintendent David Watt had tried to move Pennsy freight, and had been roughed up while trying.

Cassatt ordered a train to Pittsburgh, taking with him a telegraph operator and a lineman in case the wires should be cut en route by hostile forces. Pennsy superintendent Peterson was now also on the scene. He had several trains fired up and ready to go, with crews willing to move them, but adamant, angry strikers stood on the tracks. Pittsburgh Sheriff Fife had no success in getting the men off the tracks. When he threatened to use militia, the cry of 'Bread or blood!' filled the air.

Pennsylvania Governor Hartranft was on a junket in the West, and Lieutenant Governor James Latta joined Pennsy President Scott in bombarding him with telegrams. Finally, sensing a crisis situation, Latta ordered Pennsylvania National Guard Major General Alfred Pearson to Pittsburgh with three divisions. Of these, one went to guard the stockyards and the other two fraternized with the crowd—many of whom were their friends and relatives

Latta's sole communique from Hartranft had been 'spare nothing to protect all persons in their rights under the Constitution of the State, in accordance with the policy heretofore adopted. Am on the train to Oregon.' In other words, 'It's in your hands, congratulations! See you later.'

On the 21st, the militia were ordered to hold the 28th Street crossing, a mile east of Union Station—where, at 3 pm, more National Guard troops arrived from Philadelphia under the command of Major General Robert M Brinton.

William Thaw, a railroad director and local steel magnate, was joined by James Park Jr, another important Pittsburgh businessman, in a plea to Alexander Cassatt. They felt that the Pennsy vice president should bargain with the strikers. Cassatt felt the time for bargaining was past.

Pearson and Brinton conferred while the latter's men were gulping coffee after their miserable all-night journey from Philadelphia. They had been rousted from sleep for this duty, and en route, strike sympathizers had stoned their cars, which now displayed the dents

The Pittsburgh Riots: Shown *above* are dozens of damaged engines amid the remains of the roundhouse in which the militia had taken shelter, after the unfortunate killings which took place earlier that day. Many of the Pennsy's wooden freight cars that were on the scene burnt completely (inset), leaving only wheeltrucks on the twisted tracks.

and pockmarks of 'hearty welcomes' in various locations.

On the hill overlooking the 28th Street crossing, thousands of men, women and children had gathered to watch this rather novel entertainment. Cheering as the troops arrived, hoping to unnerve them by a show of mock support, then jeering, and then ominously silent, they were about to become more than spectators.

Brinton's men from Philadelphia marched four abreast down the tracks, with two Gatling guns in tow, toward the 28th Street crossing. The crowd now consisted of strikers, mill and factory hands, miners and thrillseekers who had gravitated to this scene of high tension.

Cassatt was nearly ill with the contradiction of his position: he had known many of the men who now struck against him; he'd advised against many of the policies that generated this very situation; but he was loyal and bound to protect the property of his railroad, and the troops were in a difficult position. Reports from witnesses that day had him stalking across the tops of

In that minute and a half of gunfire, nearly 20 workingmen died. The mob dispersed temporarily. As darkness descended over Pittsburgh, the Philadelphia troops were ordered into the roundhouse at 26th Street. Fifteen of the troops had been injured, and three more rioters had been killed trying to commandeer a field piece.

Cassatt might have been thinking back to a conversation he'd had with Pennsy General Manager Frank Thomson, after hearing of the second 10 percent wage cut. Cassatt had been angry, saying 'Why, the men cannot buy butter for their bread!' Thomson replied that they could do with meat drippings, or 'dip' as it was called. A bitter worker overheard this conversation, saying loudly that they would make do with dip, and they would fight on dip.

Now, the Philadelphia militiamen, the 'First City Company' of the National Guard, were surrounded by an angry mob. The mob tried to burn the roundhouse, but the soldiers were able to extinguish the fires. The crowd fired sporadic volleys of gunfire at the roundhouse window, and busied themselves with burning other buildings in the yard, and set fire to the extensive rolling stock in the yard. Cassatt was there, too, and was finally persuaded to leave the besieged roundhouse. He left only to scrounge up first aid and food for the soldiers, which he would be unable to get to them until the next day.

The Steel Town Lit with Flames

Eventually the roundhouse was uncontrollably ablaze—as everything else was in its vicinity—and on the morning of Sunday the 22nd, the troops marched out, dogged by the crowd. They were refused entrance to the US arsenal, so they crossed the Allegheny River, bullets fired from the crowd occasionally ricocheting around their feet.

They ate for the first time in a day. Cassatt is credited with having gotten them the food—apparently, he was able to move about quite at will, despite being well known by many of the workers.

The burning and destruction continued until evening that day, fueled somewhat by whiskey from one of the plundered trains. Union Station and Hotel had been burned; a grain elevator, all the shops, offices, engine houses and depots—39 buildings in all—had been destroyed. Passenger cars destroyed totalled 46, freight cars destroyed totalled 506; the lines west of Pittsburgh suffered the destruction of 20 passenger cars and 861 freight cars. Besides this, and of course the contents of the freight cars, 104 locomotives were wrecked—for a total estimated damages figure of $5 million.

The investigating committee that was formed to probe the incident found no fault with Cassatt's actions as the ranking Pennsy official on the scene.

The committee did, however, state that '...the capitalist himself has not been blameless. He should meet the workers halfway. The Pennsylvania was responsible only in so far as the order to send out the doubleheaders and the reduction of wages had brought on the violence.'

Some sources claim that Pennsy president Scott's involvement in the Credit Mobilier scandal was the reason

train cars, close to the action, watching every move.

Brinton's men formed a hollow square around the 28th Street depot as the crowd came closer, closer. These 'soldiers' were lawyers, businessmen and shopkeepers most of the time: their tenseness must have been on par with that of the crowd, who suffered from years of arrogant treatment by the Scott-run railroad.

As the first showers of rocks came, the soldiers held their ground. Someone fired a pistol, and as the people lunged in, attempting to grab the weapons out of their hands, the soldiers started firing: some into the crowd, but most above their heads, unwittingly into the hillside covered with people.

for his seeming 'blinders on' approach to the affair. Scott himself denied that there was any worker dissatisfaction previous to the riot. This was not strictly true— there had been a complaint presented to Scott some time before the actual outburst of troubles, but he did not respond. The Texas & Pacific Railroad figured in this— the theory that Scott was scraping Pennsy funds to feed this scheme. The theory goes that Scott needed financing to fund the Texas & Pacific, got involved in the dicey railroad investment world of the early 1870s, got stung, as nearly everybody else got stung when the bubble burst, and found himself robbing Peter— the workers— to pay Paul— the various investments, including the T&P, that he and probably the Pennsy itself had gotten caught up in.

Scott had in fact taken leave of the Pennsy to be president of the Union Pacific from 1871–1872. Scott and several associates managed to buy a controlling interest in both the Texas & Pacific and in the Trans Continental Railroad Company, and consolidated these holdings under the name Texas & Pacific Railroad Company. They organized another company, the California & Texas Railroad Construction Company, with a capital of $10 million to build the T&P trackage, which eventually ran from just south of El Paso to New Orleans. When the Panic of 1873 struck, Scott was trying to raise investors in Europe, and nearly secured the capital to cover the T&P's then outstanding debt, which was nearly $7 million. News of the Panic and the Credit Mobilier scandal broke in Europe, and Scott's investors fled, wallets and bankbooks firmly in hand.

It seems that Thomson had endorsed for more than $400,000 worth of this debt, which money Scott had legal recourse to get from Thomson's estate. The other endorsers had difficulty paying their notes, many of them eventually obtaining extensions of debt at seven percent interest. Thomson's investment represented a substantial amount of money for that time. It would seem plausible that Scott had not just incidentally come into the presidency of the Union Pacific any more than he had a sudden romantic fancy to invest in a railroad way down in Texas. We may never really know if the Pennsylvania Railroad Company had in fact used its very own Colonel Thomas A Scott as an undercover railroader in the hopes of forming a mega-railroad.

In 1875, a financial reorganization of the corporation allowed Scott and his partner Matthew Baird to make an offer to purchase at par value all the notes which bore their two signatures.

But Scott failed to get a construction loan from Congress to finance the continued building of the T&P. He had the very mixed pleasure of selling his interest in the T&P to Jay Gould, thereby recouping his losses.

Eventually, freight was rolling again (passenger traffic had not been halted to any serious degree). The doubleheaders were still running— which Cassatt felt was a management concern, none of the workers' business.

The men, however, had returned to work at the 10 percent reduced wage.

At right: A crewman of this Philadelphia, Baltimore & Washington 0–6–0 switcher proudly poses in his Sunday best for this May 1911 photo taken in Maryland. The Pennsy affiliate PB&W was born of a merger of the Baltimore & Potomac and the Philadelphia, Wilmington & Baltimore.

THE SCOTT YEARS

Thomas Scott

By the time of John Edgar Thomson's death, the Pennsylvania had expanded from its original Philadelphia to Pittsburgh route and was now a sprawling system with 6000 miles of trackage.

Thomas Scott was voted to the Pennsy presidency upon Thomson's death, in 1874. Of the impressive mileage gain noted above, it is hard to say which man, Thomson or Scott, was most responsible— Scott, as vice president under the brilliant but reclusive Thomson, was not only an excellent public relations man— he was handsome, witty, outgoing and possessed of an eloquence that could bowl opposition over— but he was a consummate railroad man. Scott had, in addition to his own talents, a very able underling in Alexander Cassatt.

This may perhaps be the question of who actually did the most good for the railroad, but the Pennsy had always, from the start, been operated under the predominant guiding spirit of prudence, and its board of directors seem mostly to have had good sense— the primary characteristic of any man who rose to a position of power in the Pennsy during the 19th century was definitely that he was a good railroader. This prudence stood the Pennsy firmly in the good, and if the line produced no spectacular 'barons' such as the Vanderbilts, men like Thomson, Cassatt and Scott certainly were 'baronial' in their concern for the railroad.

The Rockefeller Incident

Rockefeller's Standard Oil refined 10,000 barrels of oil per day, making it by far the largest refinery operation in the eastern US at that time. Sixty five percent of its product was shipped over Pennsy rails. In return for this lucrative freight tonnage, the Pennsy was known to have paid Standard up to $10 million in rebates in one 18 month period. The rebates paid by the Pennsy were not the only fealty paid to Standard— all of the roads carrying Standard Oil, including the New York Central, the Erie and the B&O were similarly held in Rockefeller's monopolistic grip.

The Pennsy moved its oil shipments via the Empire Transportation Company— an entity which consisted of 1000 iron tank cars for carrying crude oil, 400 'rack cars' for carrying refined oil, and the Union Pipe Line Company, which moved oil from suppliers in the northeast to rail connections via an extensive pipe line. The Empire was the fastest and most efficient oil feeder into the east coast oil markets, and Standard being the company's major supplier, officials at Empire worried that Standard's monopoly would soon lead the oil company to decide to use another carrier altogether, or even worse yet, that Rockefeller's burgeoning 'pipelines to the coast' operation might obviate the need for any rail carrier.

The Pennsy, the New York Central, the Erie and the B&O had been in fierce competition for the East Coast port trade since the late 1850s, with only a brief hiatus for the Civil War. The other warring roads felt that the Pennsy, with its subsidiary, was unfair in its exclusive control of Pittsburgh trade and had, according to many, levied very heavy freight rates on the merchants of that

Previous pages: The *Pennsylvania Limited* crosses Rockville bridge in the 1880s. The often brilliant fourth Pennsy president Thomas A Scott *(above)* had a trying tenure indeed, including rate wars, the Pittsburgh Riots and a defeat by oil baron John D Rockefeller.

city. Thus they would be all too happy to receive a greater share of the Standard Oil trade from the Pennsy, and would be glad to get it any way they could. The Empire's president, Joseph Potts, published a pamphlet proclaiming his naive and almost unbelievably self-destructive scheme to head Standard off at the pass by effecting a formal agreement with the Pennsy whereby the two rail companies would enter the oil refinery business themselves— thereby protecting the source of their lucrative oil carriage business. No doubt Rockefeller got wind of this little gem, and the officers of the Erie and the Central were probably already stretching their wallets for the increased cash flow that their soon-to-be increasing Standard business would give them; they knew that Rockefeller and his colleagues would not hesitate to take action. But $10 million was not exactly chicken feed, and neither the apparently cash-hungry Scott or Potts had reckoned on Rockefeller's top gun, Henry M Flagler, the man who was eventually to make tropical, mosquito-ridden Florida a tourist mecca. Scott naively assumed that the Standard was just a loosely organized money-making machine with no reactive impulses whatsoever.

At the time, Flagler was a Rockefeller henchman whose bold imagination balanced Rockefeller's shrewdness perfectly— together, they called a meeting with Potts, Scott and Cassatt. Pennsy Third Vice President Cassatt felt that the Empire and the Pennsy should lease the new Empire refineries to the Standard, perhaps even should sell them to a third party. Potts argued against that course of action. Rockefeller simply said that the Empire was not completely fair in their rating of Standard shipments, and that Standard refused to use a shipper who was also in competition for the oil refining business with them.

Scott refused to budge, Rockefeller no longer shipped with the Pennsy, and the Pennsy lost tremendous revenue through Scott's decision to enter the refinery business with the Empire. In June 1877, Scott cut wages for the Pennsy. The Pittsburgh strike raged, putting the Pennsy even farther away from financial well-being; in August, Scott was shaken upon learning that his railroad could not pay its dividend to stockholders that month. Cassatt was sent to the Standard offices in Cleveland to work out the Pennsy's surrender.

The deal went like this: Pennsy bought the Empire's cars, shops, piers and stations for $3 million ($2.5 million of which was in car trust certificates and $500,000 was in, interestingly, Texas & Pacific Railroad stock); and the Standard bought the Empire's pipeline system and refineries (which were in Philadelphia and New York). Of course, the Pennsy would never again get more than 50 percent of Standard's business—but it did get 47 percent, which left 21 percent each to the Erie and the NYC, with the B&O coming in lowest, with 11 percent—as the B&O had attempted to do reasonable business with some of Standard's independent competitors. Of course Standard, by gaining what it did from the Empire, came into a complete monopoly on oil-gathering facilities in the East, and thereby had producers, transporters and independent refiners at its mercy. Rockefeller smiled coolly. Some of the minor terminology in the agreement indicated that the Pennsy would have to pay the Standard rebates for Standard's business, plus rebates for *any oil shipped by any of the Standard's competitors.* Cassatt complained mightily in private about the arrangement—he had always hated the rebate system, and when he came into the presidency at the Pennsy, he would do something about it. For the moment, though, when John D Rockefeller had you, he had you.

Rockefeller himself described Scott's signing of the contract in Philadelphia's St George Hotel: 'I can see him now, with his big soft hat, marching into the room in that little hotel to meet us; not to sweep us away as he had always done, but coming in with a smile, walking right up to the cannon's mouth.'

Scott had been severely weakened by his dealings with Rockefeller, and left the presidency of the Pennsy in 1880. In 1881, he relinquished his presidency in the Texas & Pacific as well.

Unequal Competition

The railroad rate wars were made possible by the lack of rates regulation prior to 1887 and were not to abate entirely until the era of full regulation. The method of setting freight charges and passenger fares was entirely competitive. While these battles among the nation's railroads did benefit some of the roads capitalistically, not all roads were able or willing to continue these wars. In particular, in 1874 HJ Jewett, newly installed president of the Erie, found that the Erie could not continue to be competitive, and would shortly have to close up shop if the rate wars continued.

A meeting in Saratoga, New York was held in August of 1874, at which the presidents of the New York Central, the Pennsy and the Erie were present. They agreed to abolish objectionable practices such as rebating, and established a three-man commission which was to oversee the setting of moderate, yet adequate, rates which would satisfy the needs of all railroads concerned.

The agreement did continue a differential payment plan which favored the B&O and the Pennsy over the NYC in respect to freight rates paid by customers to the respective home ports of the three roads. The financial world of New York felt that the NYC had sold out to its competitors by going along with such an arrangement. The committee, therefore, was beginning its tenure with that particular dispute eating away at the foundation of the railroad's rating truce. Not only that, but the Grand Trunk refused any degree of participation, as it was in an extremely unstable financial state. Though this road was not important per se, it could inflict severe damage rates-wise to the other railroads, as it was in receivership, and had, so to speak, 'nothing to lose.'

Rates Slashers

A battle between the Pennsy and the B&O—concerning the very low rates the B&O was charging over its newly completed route to Chicago, and the Pennsy's handling of B&O cars and equipment when the latter were being moved over the trackage of the United Railways of New Jersey—erupted a few months after the committee had actually started functioning. These disputes were resolved in June of 1875, but the compromise resolution severely weakened the original agreement.

Meanwhile the Grand Trunk was busy slashing rates. The city of New York was greatly alarmed by the diversion of freight to Boston that these lower rates caused— at one point, the rates for freight shipped from Boston to Chicago were 50 percent lower than those from New York to Chicago. 'Commodore' Vanderbilt rose to the occasion, various conferences were convened, promises were made; promises were immediately broken. The railroads seemed to have no self-control; it was almost as if, for every road that obeyed the agreements, there was at least one that saw the situation as a chance to get the jump on the competition.

The passenger fare from Boston to Chicago dropped from over 25 dollars to 14 dollars in just a few weeks. Freight rates on produce going from Chicago to New York fell by nearly two-thirds and freight rates east to west fell to less than one-half the normal levels.

News From the South

All of the major roads involved suffered severe financial damage as a result of this, and the opinion was that such tremendous waste was to be avoided in the future. An answer to this problem came, temporarily, from the South. Colonel Albert Fink, the former vice president of the Louisville & Nashville Railroad, had organized a rates pooling association that set definite and equable

Above: A Philadelphia & Reading Camelback. Such small railroads as the P&R (part of the 'Pennsy group') generally followed their larger affiliates in rates fluctuations, and sometimes posted untenably low rates themselves. *At right:* Rail competition in the Northeast grew rapidly during the Civil War; compare this map— of most northeastern railroads extant in 1860— with the turn-of-the-century maps of just the Pennsylvania and the Vanderbilt railroad groups on page 51.

freight percentages for some 30 southern railroads and ferry lines.

It was a successful answer to such a problem as the northerners had, and in 1877, Fink was hailed northward to the state of New York to help the northern trunk lines to work out their differences. A pooling association was organized whereby the percentages of westbound freight out of New York were set as follows. Thirty-three percent of the freight went to the NYC, the same amount went to the financially ailing Erie, 25 percent went to the Pennsy, and nine percent went to the B&O— these percentages being based on each road's normal percentage of the freight business. Any road that found itself with something over this allotted percentage of westbound freight had to turn the excess over to be divided equably among the other roads involved in the agreement. The port differential arrangement was also dissolved.

Pooling of freight moving from west to east was more difficult because it was less controllable, due to the previous non-participation of the western railroads. Nevertheless, in 1879, it was attempted. At first, the western roads would not comply with the eastern roads' pooling agreements, but eventually the eastern roads stood firm. The Pennsy, the B&O, the NYC and the Erie took the lead, and the western roads were forced to cooperate.

This kind of pooling applied to other situations, and it eventually led to a power clique among the railroads— or so it was perceived by the public; who could break the grip of railroad management on the way America moved its goods? These kinds of questions hastened federal regulation, the first serious note of which was struck by the creation in 1887 of the Interstate Commerce Commission to oversee all public transport, and to regulate trade and shipping practices in the continental US. The rate wars were to continue, but the fruit borne by them was public resentment and growing federal distrust.

THE ROBERTS YEARS

Roberts Over Cassatt

The Pennsylvania's board of directors elected George B Roberts as Thomas Scott's successor in 1880. Roberts was a hardworking, dependable 'company man'. His family were Quakers, and Roberts had a quiet, even-handed approach to business that had earned him respect.

From 1851 to 1862, Roberts worked as an engineer. He was hired by J Edgar Thomson to assist with the difficult line over the Alleghenies, went on to the Sunbury and Erie, and thence to a number of the Pennsy's branch lines, to move up rapidly to the newly created office of fourth vice president in 1873, moving on to second vice president in 1873, and becoming Scott's vice president in 1874.

His election to the presidency caused some dissatisfaction—Alexander Cassatt was notably upset, and promised to resign; he felt that Roberts was fine as an executive, but lacked the force needed to guide the now-huge Pennsy over the turbulent waters of the latter 19th century.

Battle With the B&O

John W Garrett, president of the B&O, was disturbed that his railroad had no direct route to New York—if it had, he would then no longer have to pay the Pennsy for the privilege of moving freight to and from that port. Both the Pennsy and the B&O had to link up with the Philadelphia, Wilmington & Baltimore, which was the middle link in the chain across New Jersey formed by the United Railroads, the PW&B and, optionally, either the Pennsy's Baltimore & Potomac or the B&O's Washington branch.

Using the Reading line, Garrett secretly began to build an alternate route east from Philadelphia, north to the Central Railroad of New Jersey, which would extend B&O access—free the Pennsy's influence—to the west bank of the Hudson. On 1 December 1880, Garrett announced that the B&O would withdraw all its passenger trains from the Pennsy's New Jersey lines, and would follow that action by the removal of its freight cars as of January of 1881. In February of 1881, Jay Gould was elected president of the Central Railroad Company of New Jersey; a combination of Gould and Garrett meant trouble to Pennsy's access to New York. The only answer was to consolidate. The Pennsy would have to gain control of its middle line, the PW&B.

Of course, Garrett, with a consortium of Gould, John Jacob Astor and others, would try to block such an attempt. The PW&B was owned by a group of investors in Boston. After Garrett's approach, the Boston financiers offered to sell him a controlling interest in the PW&B as of March 1881.

Before Thomas Scott retired, he advised Roberts to let Cassatt do the dealing with the likes of Garrett (for whom Scott had an informed distrust), saying, 'Mr Cassatt, I think, understands the question very thoroughly and will quickly see the necessity of meeting the enemy on all points.' At one point, Cassatt was invited to join the Garrett syndicate for a one-third share in the PW&B—an obvious slap in the face, and an attempt to humiliate the Pennsy—and at another point, Garrett burst into the Pennsy Philadelphia offices to assert to Roberts and Cassatt that 'we have secured the control of the Philadelphia, Wilmington & Baltimore railroad. We are not disposed, however, to disturb your relations with the property and you need not give yourself any uneasiness on that score.' Cassatt and Roberts listened impassively to this outburst, knowing all the while that quite the opposite was true; Cassatt had gone to the Boston owners of the PW&B, after they had sent a query to the Pennsy offices; Garrett's offer of $70 per share was not enough—would the Pennsy offer more? Immediately after Garrett left the Pennsy office, Cassatt went to New York, where he contacted the investors in Boston with an offering of $78 per share for a block of 98,000 shares which Garrett had overlooked. He promised them the same price for the remaining controlling stock if they would deliver it by April 1 of that year. The Bostonians eagerly dropped Garrett's offer, and Cassatt wrote a check for $14,999,999—the largest single American business transaction to that date.

The Pennsy asked for the money to back the check the very next day, at the annual board of directors' meeting. The directors voted affirmatively. Roberts told the board that the transaction had been financed by the sale of $10 million in trust certificates. The company's stockholders concurred with the purchase, approving the release of an additional 400,000 shares of Pennsy stock, which would put $20 million more into the company coffers.

The cost of the final transaction was $17,032,879. The B&O was forced to complete its alternate route, which could not be accomplished—due to the extremely competitive conditions existent in 1881–1882—until 1886. As of 1884, the PW&B had refused to handle B&O rolling stock, and despite a lawsuit, the PW&B prevailed.

More War

With the purchase of the PW&B, the Pennsylvania became the largest industrial employer in the United States; the road employed 95,000 people and hauled 160 million tons of freight yearly. The secret rebates given to Standard were a plague upon the Pennsy, though, as was the Vanderbilt practice of lowering rates on the New York Central—the rate wars were still on, and the Pennsy leadership was at odds. Cassatt felt that some form of government regulation was needed to control the ruinous rate wars, and his chief, Roberts, felt that the idea was absurd.

New York was not finished with the Pennsy. In 1883, the Central began its scheme to promote the South Pennsylvania Railroad Company. This line began as the Duncannon, Landisburg and Broad Top Railroad Company, incorporated in 1854 to run in a general westerly direction from Harrisburg to Broad Top Mountain—thus accessing Bedford County's bituminous coal fields. The railroad had no backers, and thus was not built, but its charter had been kept alive, and several amendments later the road's charter expanded its original area of operations to include a proposed rail line from Harrisburg, running westward to the Monongahela River near Pittsburgh.

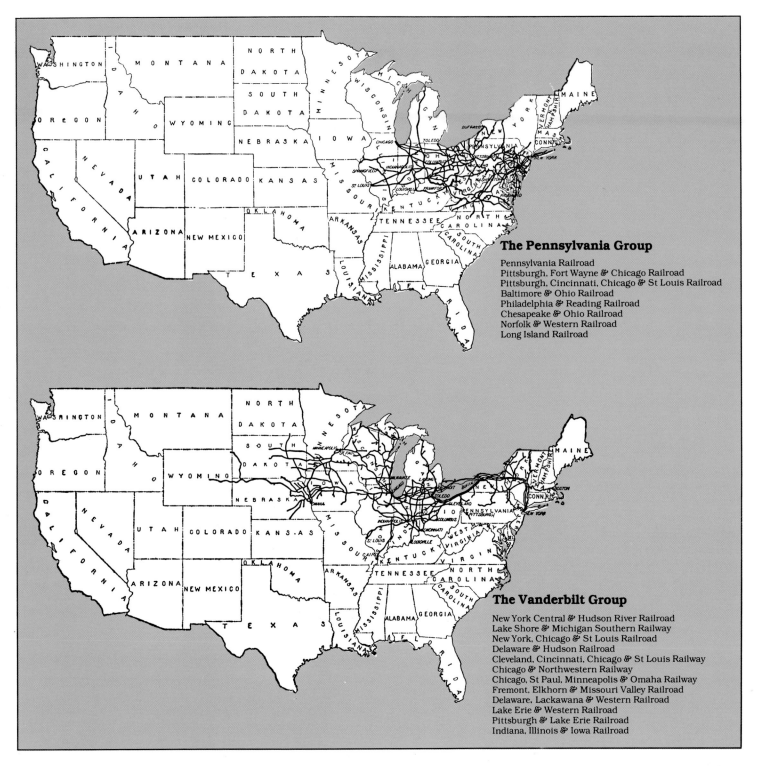

The Pennsylvania Group

Pennsylvania Railroad
Pittsburgh, Fort Wayne & Chicago Railroad
Pittsburgh, Cincinnati, Chicago & St Louis Railroad
Baltimore & Ohio Railroad
Philadelphia & Reading Railroad
Chesapeake & Ohio Railroad
Norfolk & Western Railroad
Long Island Railroad

The Vanderbilt Group

New York Central & Hudson River Railroad
Lake Shore & Michigan Southern Railway
New York, Chicago & St Louis Railroad
Delaware & Hudson Railroad
Cleveland, Cincinnati, Chicago & St Louis Railway
Chicago & Northwestern Railway
Chicago, St Paul, Minneapolis & Omaha Railway
Fremont, Elkhorn & Missouri Valley Railroad
Delaware, Lackawana & Western Railroad
Lake Erie & Western Railroad
Pittsburgh & Lake Erie Railroad
Indiana, Illinois & Iowa Railroad

The Reading Railroad's line ran from Philadelphia through Reading to Harrisburg, and had no link to the West. In the late 1870s, Reading president Franklin B Gowen saw the South Penn's possibilities for the Reading—if it were built. However, in May 1880, the Reading went into receivership and the South Penn again lay dormant. Gowen was made receiver of the Reading, and contacted William Vanderbilt *in re* the possibilities of the Reading/South Penn access to Pennsylvania's coal fields and its direct route to that Pennsylvania Railroad stronghold, Pittsburgh. Pittsburgh itself was overjoyed when the news broke that Vanderbilt and Gowen were forming a syndicate to construct the new route. Andrew Carnegie, who had himself been a fast rising young executive with the Pennsy back in the 1860s, was one of the largest subscribers to the syndicate—he envisioned lower rates for his expanding steel empire—and his col-

Previous pages: The Pennsy's Harrisburg station in 1870. *Above:* These maps trace the competitive trackage of the Pennsy and the New York Central/Vanderbilt group. Note the comparatively convoluted nature of the Pennsy, and the ranginess of the NYC group. The Pennsy came to epitomize line traffic increases by way of multi-tracking.

league in the steel industry, Henry Oliver, followed suit. Many other Pittsburghians jumped on the bandwagon, anxious to be free of Pennsy 'rate tyranny,' as they called it.

Exhaustive surveys were made, and the line finally laid out for construction was 30 miles shorter than the analogous Pennsy line, but had steeper grades and was to cross the Alleghenies at an elevation 285 feet higher than the Pennsy lines. A bond issue was made by which the Reading and the NYC would guarantee the interest on 20 million dollars' worth of the proposed railroad's bonds. Contracts were let out for bridge construction over the Susquehanna. Work went well and a completion date was set—for 1 July 1886—in early 1885. J Pierpont Morgan had recently made a big splash when he sold a large block of New York Central bonds on the London market. His expertise in railroad investments gave him a sure knowledge of public attitudes toward investing in railroad securities, both domestically and on the foreign markets. He felt that American railroads were headed for disaster, that their cutthroat attitudes were suicidal; no one would dare to invest in such unstable entities as American railroads were fast becoming in the eyes of the world.

Morgan to the Rescue

Morgan, upon hearing of the South Penn Railroad imbroglio, called New York Central and Pennsylvania Railroad executives together for a meeting, at which he undoubtedly told them what fools they were making of themselves. An agreement was reached whereby Mr Morgan acquired the right to sell a 60 percent controlling interest in South Penn bonds to the Pennsy, and the Pennsy would give the owners of the South Penn $5.6 million in three percent bonds of the Bedford and Bridgeport Railroad Company. The NYC had also planned a cut into Pennsylvania coal fields by way of the Beech Creek Railroad, which ran from Williamsport west to Clearfield, directly paralleling the Philadelphia & Erie. This gambit was also countered in the Morgan negotiations—the Pennsy gained control of the Beech Creek on mutually agreeable terms.

Work on the South Penn was discontinued on September 12 and was never taken up again. The state of Pennsylvania felt that this wheeling and dealing was out of hand—and no doubt some very serious lobbying had been done by the Pittsburgh merchant class—whereby the state brought an injunction against the Pennsy, taking the Beech Creek out of its hands and restoring it to the New York Central. The South Pennsy could go back to its syndicate too, but no one endeavored to reinstate building the road. Most of its equipment was sold at auction in 1890, and the Pennsy, enjoined from satisfying its original obligations concerning the South Penn, made a 'conscience payment' of $1.8 million—including lawyer's fees and interest dating from 1 February 1889—on 4 March 1892.

Cassatt Retires

Giving added strength to this boast, Alexander Cassatt had a pet project. He resigned as Pennsy's first vice president on 2 September 1882, ostensibly to spend more time with his family, and to spend more time with his horses, which he loved. But he was not done with the Pennsy; on 12 September 1883, Cassatt was elected to the Pennsy board of directors.

A Special Line to Dixie

Turning toward the nation's South, the New York, Philadelphia & Norfolk line extended the Philadelphia, Wilmington & Baltimore line down the Delmarva (Delaware/Maryland/Virginia) Peninsula to Cape Charles, Virginia, and by steamer from that point to Nor-

Above: An 0–6–0 switcher at the Pennsy's mechanical heart, Altoona.

folk—thus creating a direct Pennsy route to the South, availing the Pennsy of another port and picking up on the lucrative seafood trade that flowed into it.

The NYP&N had been Scott and Cassatt's 'baby' when Scott was the Pennsy president and Cassatt his second vice president. The Pennsy board refused, for a long time, to support the construction of this line.

The NYP&N's promise eventually warmed the hearts of the board—the ever-cautious Pennsy did eventually enter into operating agreements with the NYP&N, when it had at last become clear that the road was not simply a pipe dream. The road was known informally, and widely, as 'The Cassatt Line South.'

Scott had dreamed it up, and excellent organizer that he was, he chose one of the best line engineers he could find—Alexander Cassatt. In 1881, the Pennsy, at Cassatt's prompting, purchased the charter to build such a line as the NYP&N would eventually be.

In 1882, Cassatt personally inspected the proposed route, and found that not only seafood and port business awaited its building, but rich tracts of timber lined its way to the tip of the peninsula, promising additional revenues from the lumber industry. Though pressed by local towns to run the tracks, and the line's prosperity, through them, Cassatt (probably mindful of his own wallet, which was increasingly likely at the time to be

the source of the NYP&N's building fund) drew a straight line with a ruler down the peninsula.

The ailing, retired Scott asked 'How will you transfer your freight across the Chesapeake Bay expeditiously?' Cassatt replied, 'We will build powerful and fast transfer tugs that will transport loaded trains across the bay.' Cassatt designed steel barges, with the capacity to carry 18 loaded freight cars. Cassatt approached Roberts about building the line again, but he again balked.

Scott and Cassatt were aided in their financing of the line by several acquaintances who had bought bonds in the venture. Then, in 1883, the Pennsy and the Philadelphia, Wilmington & Baltimore made an agreement to pay 20 percent of the profits from their freight interchange toward buying bonds in the NYP&N.

NYP&N tracks were built from either end of the existing Peninsula Railroad Companies' rails—north toward the Pennsylvania border, and south toward the Chesapeake Bay.

By 1 November 1883, tracks stretched to Cape Charles at the end of the peninsula. Cassatts' barges were still being built, so he hired a steamer, the *Jane Mosely*, to haul passengers and freight across the often-turbulent bay. In 1884, the line had made a net profit of $50,236.34. Cassatt went to Washington that fall, attempting to persuade the federal government to dredge a channel in the bay in order to permit the passage of his heavy low-riding barges. Both of the departments he approached—the Department of War (for the Army Corps of Engineers) and the Department of the Interior—refused.

Cassatt used his own money to finance the dredging, and by April 1885, the barges were moving, and they were very successful. Railroaders worldwide imitated this solution to rail transport over water; the Trans-Siberian Railroad used this system some years later to move its cars over Lake Baikal, for instance. In this country, Cassatt's barge system was to see extensive use on Lake Erie, transporting freight to many points in the northern central US and, internationally, to Canada.

Cassatt was made president of the NYP&N, maintaining that position until his acceptance of the presidency of the Pennsy in 1899. The Pennsy finally bought the NYP&N in 1908, and the line proved a vital link to the South for the Pennsy.

Line Extensions

As for Roberts' tenure, besides the already-mentioned expansion of the railway system, there were extensions of the Northern Central (to Lake Ontario, by purchase of the Sodus Bay & Southern RR Co, some 34 miles, which proved to be a lucrative coal road); and the Cumberland Valley (to Winchester, Virginia, by means of building branch lines). Roberts also purchased the Terre Haute & Indianapolis, which, with its subsidiaries, comprised some 467 miles of trackage. During the Roberts administration, some 1100 miles were added to the Pennsy trackage west of Pittsburgh.

All over the system, yards were being expanded and new yards were being built to accommodate the Pennsy's increased trackage. Sole ownership of the Union Railroad of Baltimore was acquired in 1881, and in 1883, the tracks of this company were elevated to eliminate grade crossings—this was to become a common, operations-efficiency gaining move throughout the Pennsy system in the years to come.

The Johnstown Flood

The Johnstown flood was a disaster without parallel in the history of the Pennsylvania Railroad. Back in the 1830s, the Main Line of Public Works had dammed the south fork of the Conemaugh River to provide a constant water supply for that system's Western Division Canal. This reservoir normally contained some 15 million tons of water. On 30 May 1889, an abnormally fierce storm dumped torrential rains on the area, and the dam's spillway could not release enough to relieve the tremendous pressure on the dam caused by the huge volumes of water which were pouring into the reservoir. On 31 May 1889, a telegrapher at South Fork, Pennsylvania tried to get a warning message of this situation to Johnstown, downstream from the Conemaugh reservoir, but was unable to do so because the storms had swamped the lines.

That very afternoon, the dam burst, all across its front, releasing a wall of water 20 feet high. Trackage for 10 miles was obliterated; 34 locomotives, 24 passenger cars and 561 freight cars were destroyed. Even locomotives were swept away by the tremendous force of the water, some of them being found more than a mile downstream. Thirty passengers were drowned and some 2500 people were killed at Johnstown, trapped in railcars, houses and caught on the streets by the flood.

More than 1600 houses and scores of shops and factories were destroyed—and as soon as the water had receded, fires started by quicklime which had been contained in some of the now-destroyed rail cars finished off what was left.

As a terrible adjunct to this, flooding east of the mountains did tremendous damage there, along with which was the loss of three Pennsy bridges in the Juniata Valley. Material costs to restore the Pennsy facilities in the area to minimal operating condition amounted to $3,475,425.01.

Passenger service was fully restored as of 24 June 1889 and freight service was restored as of July 17 of that year. The following is an excerpt from a contemporary account of the deaths of 26 people aboard the Pennsy *Day Express:*

'...There was no time for explanation and none was needed. No time for lingering farewell, last kiss and fond caress. Already the roar of the advancing waters filled the air. Those who first reached the platform saw wrecked houses, broken bridges, trees and rocks borne on a tidal wave just turning the bend three hundred yards away. Frantic exertions were made to escape to the protecting hills back of the station. An old mill-race, never filled up, was in the way, with narrow planks for crossings. Some of the terrified passengers jumped or fell into the waters and drowned, the deluge from the reservoir overtaking them as they floundered in the ditch. A few of those who could not leave the train survived with painful bruises, a drenching and a paralyzing fright, the waters rising half-way to the car-roofs. Several were caught in the deadly swirl as they tried to crawl under the vestibuled coaches of the second section, which lay on the inside track.

...An ominous roar and the round-house and nine heavy engines disappeared. Everything in the line of the flood was displaced or swallowed up. Locomotives were tossed aside and their tenders spirited off. A baggagecar of the mail train broke its couplings and drifted out of view, while the rear car swung around at right angles to the track. A pullman coach rolled off and was crushed, a resident picking up one of its gas fixtures next day at the lower end of Woodvale. Mere playthings for the whirlpool, engines and cars were hidden beneath timbers, brush and dirt. Slaked by the water, a cargo of lime on the train between the sections of the express set two Pullman coaches blazing. Thus fire and flood combined to lend fresh horrors to the onslaught. The coaches burned to the trucks...'

Frank Thomson

George B Roberts suffered from a chronic cardiac valve misfunction which was the side effect of a bout with typhoid fever he'd had while helping to engineer the Pennsy's Mountain Division. In August 1896, Pennsy president Roberts had a massive heart attack, and after a prolonged struggle to recover, died in January of 1897. He was 64 years old, and was well-respected, even by his arch-rival, Chauncey Depew, president of the New York Central, who esteemed him thusly:

'He appreciated, as few do, the relations of the railways to the public...He brought his company to the peak of efficiency, and was...the master of the business...'

Roberts was succeeded by Frank Thomson. Thomson had succeeded AJ Cassatt as Second Vice President of the Pennsy when the latter had retired from that position in 1882. Thomson had the rotten luck to come into the presidency just as the 'Free Silver' advocates were mounting their threat against the national monetary standard. Freight rates, because of this unstable situation, were at an all-time low.

Thomson had his accomplishments, though; he established standardized construction procedures for all aspects of the Pennsy physical plant—an undertaking that was to have a lasting beneficial effect, in terms of safety of construction and materials costs saved, on the Pennsy and its subsidiaries for years to come. Unfortunately, Frank Thomson died at the age of 58, on 5 June 1899. Some sources say that the strain of presiding over such a massive entity as the Pennsy during such economically troubled times literally had cost Thomson his life. Whether this view is merely romantic, or an accurate window on the difficulties of the Pennsy presidency at the time, Thomson's death gave Alexander Cassatt the opportunity to manifest perhaps the most spectacular achievements in Pennsy history.

Above: On 30 May 1893, the Walter Mains Circus left Clearfield, Pennsylvania en route to an engagement on the other side of the mountains. At Little Horseshoe Curve—the baby brother of Horseshoe Curve (see page 67)—near Tyrone, Pennsylvania, the train derailed, causing the deaths of 100 animals and six people.

Railroading in the mountains could be dangerous. The Pennsy ever emphasized upkeep and maintenance. The road also tended toward sparer, huskier motive power than other railroads, preferring the solidity of frame and stability of simpler, more efficient designs. Still, as shown here, accidents could and would happen.

FREIGHT AND PASSENGER
SERVICE; LOCOMOTIVES

Freight

The first freight cars were four-wheel boxes. Use of eight-wheel cars, the cars being mounted on Ross Winans' patented swiveling trucks, commenced in the 1840s, and was common in the 1850s, the eight-wheelers completely replacing the four-wheelers by the 1870s.

The cars were of a number of types—'platform' cars, which are now called 'flatcars'; and 'house' cars, which are now called 'boxcars.' Coal cars officially entered the Pennsy roster in 1857. Iron wheel trucks first came into use in 1863, beginning a gradual replacement on all Pennsy rolling stock of the then old-fashioned wooden trucks. In the late 1870s, car suspensions were changed from rubber blocks to semi-elliptical springs—which was a breakthrough, the springs providing a much more manageable ride.

Gondola cars were first built in 1868, and 'cabin' cars appeared for the first time in 1870. Brakes were due for an improvement—the old system braked only one truck set of wheels per car. With the advent of better braking systems, especially the Westinghouse air brake (see 'Pennsy Lines Locomotives'), this disaster-provoking situation improved drastically, it having been seen that stopping the cars was at least as important as moving them.

The Pennsy pioneered in the use of Janney automatic couplers in 1882. The old coupling system had been of the link and pin variety, and made connecting cars a process which took time and risked injury to the man who had to stand between the cars, as they were being brought together, in order to couple them. The Janney coupler eliminated most of the 'personal' contact of man and machine, and in the process the switching yard casualty count went down and the time it took to make up trains lessened appreciably.

George Westinghouse had an invention on the drawing board that was to greatly reduce the mechanical breakdown rate for freight cars. This invention was known as the friction draft gear, and was designed to absorb the shock generated by the forward (or backward) tugging and pulling of the train, and was mounted on the drawbar shank. After a period of testing, and several trials of variations of this device, a satisfactory arrangement, with one key attached to a cast steel coupling yoke, came into use in 1915.

All-steel hopper gondola cars introduced general all-steel car construction, a trend that was to become nearly universal, in 1898. Due to the strong new material, car sizes and weight capacities increased steadily from that point; one example of the newer, stronger equipment being the Pennsy's mid-20th century mammoth four-truck super flatcar, which was capable of carrying 400 tons.

One interesting sidelight to the story of the Pennsy freight business is that, during World War I, there came to be a shortage of freight cars which mounted to as high as 144,797 for all US railroads in 1917. This was not because there were not enough cars; the cars were simply not available—the Merchant Marine had too few ships and could not move the huge quantities of freight being sent across the ocean. Freight cars were piling up, not to be unloaded for months, in East Coast shipyards.

As soon as the US properly entered the war, the nation's railroads agreed to cooperate with the government to expedite shipments. The Special Committee on National Defense was set up, with presidents of 28 railroads presiding on its board. These chose an executive committee of five which was known as the Railroad's War Board. Fairfax Harrison of the Southern Railway, Julius Kruttschnitt of the Southern Pacific, Hale Holden of the Burlington, Howard Elliott of the Northern Pacific and Samuel Rea, president of the Pennsy were on that board. Also acting in cooperation with the board was Edgar Clark of the Interstate Commerce Commission. Despite the Board's success—freight tonnage rose from 365 billion tons in 1916 to 394 billion tons moved in late 1917—US President Wilson ordered an emergency wartime government takeover of the railroads in a move that was to create great difficulty, if not spell the beginnings of a deadly trend, for the nation's railroads.

The Pennsy's Enola freight yard, across the Susquehanna from Harrisburg, was the world's largest freight yard in the 1940s. One of Cassatt's many 'improvements' made in the early 1900s, this yard grew from its original layout as a switching yard having 12 tracks to a behemoth with over 140 miles of tracks controlled by 476 switches. The eastbound classification yard could handle 2668 cars, and the westbound classification yard could accommodate 3428 cars; the eastbound receiving yard could hold 1948 cars, the westbound receiving yard could process 1721 cars, and the container yard could take care of 140 cars. During World War II, as many as 20,000 cars passed through the Enola yard per day, and previous to the war, the yard would often handle as many as 10,000 cars per day.

The Pennsy incorporated the use of modern conveniences for coordinating switch operations, locomotives and car movements within their freight yards throughout the Pennsy system. Loudspeaker systems announced general orders and 'paged' crewmembers and yard personnel; telephones installed in engine cabs enabled engineers and dispatchers to better facilitate the connection of locomotives and cars; teletype machines got the word out and brought it in from points outside the yard, ensuring that the proper order of shipments—as handed down from points east or west—would take place.

In 1946, the Pennsy's freight traffic totalled 13 percent of all that in the nation, and yards such as the Pitcairn near Pittsburgh, and others dotted here and there throughout the Pennsy system, assisted the Enola yard in the handling of the Pennsy's intensive freight traffic. The average yard handled as many as 9000 cars per day—about 88 trains per day—and in World War II, the peak was perhaps 9800 cars per day.

The Pennsy's freight stock reached its peak in the years 1913-1919, with 282,729 units in the latter year. Overall freight tonnage continued to grow, however, due to the development of freight cars with larger capacities, and reached its peak in 1931 at 14.7 million tons total for the year. The changeover from wooden to steel cars greatly facilitated the streamlining of the overall Pennsy

Previous pages: A Pennsy 4-4-0 American—the ubiquitous design of the 19th century. *Right and above right:* Early steel freight cars. The upright brake wheels on these cars set the brakes for parking.

freight fleet: steel cars could be built to carry more tons per car—therefore, fewer cars could do what many had been doing. This changeover occurred between 1900 and 1925.

Approximately one-third of all ore shipments on the Great Lakes were moved by the Pennsy. Docks at Ashtabula, Cleveland and Erie primarily handled ore and coal, with ore being the predominate incoming burdenage (feeding US steel mills), and coal being the predominate outgoing cargo. Barges and tugs bore the Pennsy name and logo.

At Cleveland, special ore loading facilities existed which enabled ore to be taken directly from the barge and dumped directly into the waiting hopper cars. The versatile Cleveland machines were also used to unload the ore into storage piles, to build up a surplus usable in winter, when the Great Lakes were by and large closed to shipping, due to inclement weather and ice. The Cleveland ore facility could load 60 tons—an entire hopper car—in one minute.

Passenger Service

Previous to 1872, the Pennsy used a through route from Jersey City to Chicago which was known as the 'Allentown Route.' This route, actually 12 miles shorter than the Philadelphia direct to Chicago route which replaced it, featured 'Silver Palace Sleeping Cars,' the first luxury passenger accommodations on the Pennsy. These were manufactured by George Pullman's Palace Car Company (incorporated in 1867), and featured ex-

terior trim of ornately carved wood and 'palatial' richly colored paint.

The Pennsy's arch-rival, the New York Central, had sleepers, too, but these were (one could say appropriately) manufactured by George Pullman's chief rival in the sleeping car trade, Webster Wagner. This situation might be called a 'double rivalry'—Pennsy/Pullman versus NYC/Wagner, the type of situation that has often occurred in the annals of our mercantile society. The Allentown Route closed in 1867, when the United Railroads of New Jersey complex was formed, and negotiations were started by which the URRNJ was finally acquired by the Pennsy in 1871. The Silver Palace cars themselves begat a lineage of passenger accommodations. Pullman cars included diners with full kitchens, smoking lounges, card rooms, barber shops, beauty salons, libraries and of course very luxurious sleepers.

In the beginning, passenger cars were constructed much like stage coaches, eventually evolving toward the now familiar lozenge, or rectangle, shape. The Camden & Amboy was the first road to use wheel trucks on its cars; each truck had six wheels, and this equipment was standard C&A equipment until its acquisition by the Pennsy in 1871. The first car with a center aisle was used on C&A tracks, in obvious one-upmanship over the standard 'theater seat' arrangement of the day. The 'aisle car' was built in New Brunswick in 1838, and led to further experimentation, until the now-common aisle seating arrangement was achieved in 1843. The seats of C&A cars were improved in 1850, with seat backs that could be reversed to provide front or rear facing seating

arrangements at the whim of the passengers. The C&A was known to have the best passenger cars of its time.

The *Chambersburg* was the first sleeping car ever built for a railroad. It went to work for the Cumberland Valley in the spring of 1838.

The first passenger stock used on the Pennsy was authorized on 26 April 1848– this equipment consisted of two passenger cars and one baggage car: the passenger cars being little more than long boxes lined on either side by six-paned windows.

Frequent loss of luggage and property claims lodged against the Pennsy resulted from the 'help yourself' baggage handling system used in the early days. A baggage check system wherein identification tags were fashioned of metal disks which were then attached to passenger baggage was used. A duplicate of this metal tag was given to the passenger. The baggage check system of cardboard and plastic tags which we use today evolved directly from that early Pennsy system.

Pennsy baggagemen in the 1860s often had to serve as brakemen, too– those being the days before air braking systems applied the brakes throughout a train uniformly. Brakemen had to apply the brakes on each car individually, so, in addition to keeping passenger car lamps lit (another baggageman duty), the baggageman had to 'attend a brake on, or nearest to, the baggage car.'

Years before the advent of baggage cars on the Pennsy proper, the Camden & Amboy had developed a 'container' method of baggage handling. Because passenger goods had to be handled four times during the New York-Philadelphia journey (due to boat connections that had to be made at both ends of the route), wheeled containers approximately six feet by four feet were filled with luggage, and when loading from boat to railroad, the containers were hauled off the boat by mules, wheeled to the train and ramped into flatcars coupled to the head of the train; for boat connections, the containers were off-ramped from the cars, wheeled to the boat, and lashed down.

In the 1850s, the Pennsy bought 10 passenger cars and three baggage cars from the Eagle & Phoenix Lines, three low grade passenger cars from Bingham & Dock for $1800, and bought the material goods and corporate reputation of Leech and Company for $5000– which material goods were, of course, passenger cars. As of July 1858, smoking cars had been added to through passenger trains. Wider cars were being used for all passenger carriers, being nine feet wide by nearly 38 feet long. Height inside the car was a low-ceiling six feet 10 and one-half inches in the center, sloping to six feet, five inches along the sides.

Suspended candle lamps provided illumination, and box stoves provided warmth in early sleepers. Pullman would later improve on sleeper cars by such physical plan enhancements as sleeping berths which could be hoisted out of the way during the day by means of ropes and pulleys, making his sleepers convertible to day

Below left: In an August 1945 photo, a Pennsy boxcab electric is about to draw its commuter train abreast of the switchtower at Wawa, Pennsylvania. *Below:* The first GG-1 powered version of the Pennsy special the *Metropolitan* arrives at Harrisburg station in 1938.

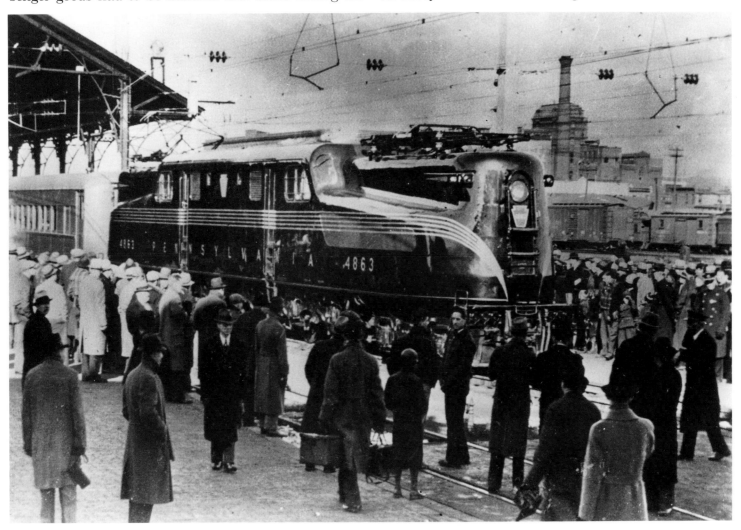

coaches complete with bench seating. Incorporating the upper berth feature and convertible seats for the lower tier of passenger accommodations was the *Pioneer*, which became a part of Abraham Lincoln's funeral train.

At any rate the sleepers were a success, and after the Civil War, railroads such as the Pennsy contracted to lease Pullman cars for their passenger trains. As mentioned at the beginning of this discussion on Pennsy passenger cars, Pullman and his partner Ben Field incorporated the Palace Car Company in 1867. Pullman made a lasting impression on the American rail industry in ways other than the Pullman cars per se. The Pullman designs established not only new luxuries, but new physical dimensions as well, adding a foot and a half to the then standard six to seven-foot head clearance in the cars, 10 feet to car lengths, and increasing the then standard 9 foot car width to 10 feet, which became the standard. In fact, many stations and loading facilities had to modify their platforms to conform with the wider Pullman car width.

Steam heating for cars was introduced in 1881—the steam being generated by boilers borne in the cars themselves, and later via a steam transfer system fed by the locomotive. This system and its various modification became part of history when the Pennsy replaced its steam loco fleet with diesels in the mid-20th century.

The following is a contemporary account of a dining car designed and manufactured not by Pullman, but—as was sometimes the case—by the personnel of the Pennsylvania Railroad. This car was inaugurated on the *Pennsylvania Limited* on 6 May 1882: 'There are eight tables 3' 4" long and 3' 7" wide. The dining room proper is 24' long and 8'9" wide.The ventilators at the top of the car are separated to a much greater extent than is usual, thus making the ceiling much wider and the car much lighter and cheerful looking.

Above the handsome mahogany the clerestory windows are of stained glass. The clerestory is of curl-ash, polished like the surface of a mirror. Four large double silver chandeliers scatter abundant light through the room, reenforced on each end of the cars with four tasteful silver sconces that in three branches hold blush red wax candles. Another feature ... is the exquisite silver adorned sideboard of carved mahogany, plate glass and dark velvet plush. Opposite this ... is a wine closet, while in the rear of the dining room is the wine closet proper, containing a receptacle for ice, over which are wine racks for 125 bottles. Next to this is a parcel cupboard, and opposite a Baker steam heater, and then a large linen closet.'

The Pullman vestibule was brought into service in 1887. This bit of car architecture made it possible to pass easily from one passenger car to another by means of an enclosed passageway. This passageway was comprised of an elastic diaphragm mounted on the end of each car; when the cars were brought together, the diaphragms pressed firmly against each other.

Flat roof designs for passenger cars went by the board in the mid-1870s, with a clerestory roof extending to both ends of the cars, the windows in which were, in fancier models, stained glass—which provided additional, if muted, daytime lighting for passengers. Another advantage of the clerestory roof was that its windows (or sometimes movable opaque panels) could be hinged

Nineteenth century passenger cars. *Above opposite:* A Pullman Palace lounge car, with sleeper/daycar setup in back; note the clerestory lighting and swivel seats. *Below opposite:* A later sleeper/daycar. The berths above the seats pulled down for sleeping and folded up for daytime. Note the reversible seat backs here, which design still sees use on such as the Southern Pacific's commuter trains. *Above:* A two-decker sleeper/daycar, showing upper and lower sleepers open.

open to provide additional ventilation for passengers. Eventually, the clerestory was done away with when the first ice-activated air conditioning systems were applied to passenger cars in the 1930s. Closely following this change was an overall move toward streamlining Pennsy passenger cars. The clerestory eliminated, the cars assumed a 'round top' look, with interior headroom of 8 feet, 10 inches.

The first all-steel passenger cars were tried out by the Long Island RR in 1905. The Pennsy system being so satisfied by the results of this experiment that the company placed an order for 500 coaches with the Pullman Company. From that point on, Pullman manufactured all of its cars with steel. The Long Island's pioneering exclusive use of steel passenger cars proceeded from one of Pennsy's most spectacular feats, the construction of the Manhattan tunnels and their through point, Pennsylvania Station, in Manhattan: steel cars were thought to be better than wood for use in the Hudson River tunnels.

The next major design change since the introduction of roomy all-steel cars came in 1938. This passenger car was an electro-mechanically air conditioned car, seating 66 passengers, and was followed closely by yet another air conditioned design which seated 44 passengers

(down from 66 to make for more passenger comfort and to fit more improvements into the car's design). These 'modern' cars introduced the all-too-pervasive fluorescent lighting to rail travel, and featured rotating/reclining seats, men's and ladies' rooms, and many of the conveniences which have since become standard on passenger cars.

The use of coil springs for passenger cars provided smoother ride and better railcar handling characteristics than did the old setup, which used stiff blocks of solid rubber. These coil springs were a Pennsylvania Railroad breakthrough, and the use of them became universal in the American rail system after a few years.

Pennsy Specials

The Pennsy was the first railroad to run a 'limited' passenger train, in 1876, between Jersey City and Chicago; it was labeled a 'limited' because the number of cars, and hence, the number of passengers was limited to enable faster running. This route was upgraded, and in 1881, the *Pennsylvania Limited* made its first runs on this line, breaking previous records with a time of 26 hours and 40 minutes. This train was, and continued to be to the end of its days, remarkable for its punctuality. This very punctuality enabled the New York Central's *20th Century Limited* to adopt a similar schedule, and when the *Pennsylvania Limited* eventually became the *Broadway Limited*, the two competing trains 'raced' from Chicago to New York City, over parallel tracks for the first leg of the journey. Pulling out

of Chicago, the two trains were literally within eyesight of one another, and as their powerful locomotives pulled them, both crews and passengers were caught up in the friendly competition—a bonus that neither railroad had exactly planned on.

The finest cars yet built for a railroad were assigned to the *Pennsylvania Limited*—besides lush appointments, these cars were equipped with electric lights, and offered a full staff, including barber, stenographer and maid service.

On 15 June 1902, the *Pennsylvania Limited* became the *Pennsylvania Special*, running a 20 hour schedule between New York and Chicago behind a Pennsy Atlantic loco—the fast, dependable passenger hauler of the Pennsy lineup. The train ran four cars, with every convenience and luxury passengers could want—and had come to expect from the Pennsy. It was withdrawn from service in February 1903, but re-emerged on 11 June 1905 with an 18-hour schedule. Its first day of service saw the train hauling down a record for a westbound run that hit speeds of 127 miles per hour. This train became the *Broadway Limited* on 24 November 1912 and saw service into the Pennsy's latter years, running a regular schedule of 16 hours between New York City and Chicago. Legend has it that the *Broadway Limited* was not named for New York's famous thoroughfare, but for the wide, steel-gleaming quadruple trackbeds of the Pennsy system.

Other famous Pennsy fliers were the *Spirit of Saint Louis*, the *General*, the *Red Arrow* and—to and from New England—the *Senator* and the *Colonial*, as well as deluxe trains such as the east-west running *Jeffersonian* and *Trail Blazer.*

Inaugurated on 7 December 1885, the *Congressional Limited* ran between New York and Washington. This deluxe train had the honor of carrying many important people who were usually on very important business, running a schedule for its 225-mile line of 3 hours and 35 minutes in the 1940s.

Locomotives

By 1849, when the Pennsylvania Railroad Company set its wheels on tracks for the first time, locomotive building had already progressed considerably. Most of the basic design problems inherent in making a machine pull other machines along double ribbons of track had been surmounted, and now was the beginning of the era of improvements.

The Pennsy's first locomotives were built by the Baldwin Locomotive Works. These locos were the *Dauphin* and the *Perry.*

These were, however, not the first locos to actually go to work on the Pennsy. A locomotive, delivered later than the two above, and based on the British *Crampton*

Above left: An observation car, circa 1910. Note the booths in back, the cozy leather seats, and the cuspidors between seats, catering to the then-prevailing habit of chewing tobacco. *Above:* 'The Broad Way.' Four track lines became the Pennsy standard in the 20th century.

design, went to work first, in September 1849. This was the passenger locomotive *Mifflin*, and was also a Baldwin product. The *Mifflin* had 14 x 20-inch cylinders, a single pair of 72-inch drivers, a pair of 'carrying wheels' ahead of the drivers, and a four-wheel truck of 33-inch wheels. *Mifflin*'s carrying wheels could be moved by means of a lever situated in the engine's cab— thus transferring some of the weight borne by the carrying wheels to the drivers, in order to gain starting traction. Once the train was under way, the carrying wheels could be returned to their 'bearing' position. The *Mifflin* and its two companions in design, *Blair* and *Indiana*, which came on line in late 1849 and early 1850, respectively, were fast locomotives for their time, one of them having recorded a sustained run at a mile per minute.

The *Dauphin* and the *Perry* were freight locomotives, having four pairs of drivers and no leading truck, like later yard switcher designs. These remained in Pennsy service for a short period, then were sold to the Philadelphia & Reading, although a companion loco of the same design, the *Westmoreland*, served the Pennsy until 1860.

Many railroads found the 4-4-0 'American' locomotive to be a versatile source of motive power for their lines.

The Pennsy ordered several from Baldwin and the Norris locomotive works. The 4-4-0s, with their two sets of drivers and their four wheel leading truck, struck a very useful balance between the big-drivered Cramptons and the truckless, multi-drivered freight engines of the time, setting the standard for American locomotive design for many years to come. This design is perhaps the most well-known locomotive design of them all.

Building Steam

As of the year end 1851, the Pennsy had 26 locomotives, 23 of which were Baldwins and three of which were Norris locos. These engines ranged from having two to four (these being passenger locos) to six to eight driving wheels.

Tractive force for these engines ranged from 2600 to 11,000 pounds— at the highest, roughly one-fifth of the average tractive force that would be generated by Pennsylvania steam locomotives 100 years 'down the road.'

The Pennsy's rolling stock holdings were in a process of rapid growth, and with the acquisition of the Philadelphia & Columbia Railroad in 1857 (and the addition of that company's rolling stock to the Pennsy's roster), the road had 195 locomotives, of over 40 varying designs, with from two to eight drivers, the engines' weights varying from the lightest two-driver design— 23,350 pounds— to the heaviest eight-driver engine— 66,600

At top, above: A Pennsy 2–6–0 Mogul medium freight engine of the late 19th century. *Opposite:* A 2–8–0 Consolidation of the same era pulls a long train up the sweeping grade of spectacular Horseshoe Curve (see text, page 34). *Above:* Though the Pennsy reconfigured its Camelbacks, such of its affiliates as the Lehigh Valley used them.

pounds— with at least one six-driver machine weighing in at 67,200 pounds.

The manufacturers of these various engines, listed roughly in order of the quantities of locomotives they made for the Pennsy and its affiliates, were as follows: the Baldwin Locomotive Works, Richard Norris & Sons, Smith & Perkins, Ross Winans, Wilmarth, Lancaster and the New Jersey Manufacturing Company. Baldwin was by far the leader here, supplying approximately 48 percent of the road's locos, with Norris & Sons a distant second, supplying approximately 26 percent of the road's motive power.

The Smith & Perkins engines were 2–6–0s, and as such were design forerunners of the *Mogul* class locomotives that would be such a success in the 1860s. Norris 4–4–0 locos with 72-inch, 60-inch and 54-inch drivers were built in 1853-1854. The Norris engines were known for their speed, but were too light of frame, and their boilers were too vulnerable to shock and vibration.

Previous to 1857, Pennsy locos were known by their names. In 1857, the practice of designating locos by

name *and* number was under way, and after this, no doubt due to accounting and records-keeping practices, locomotives on the Pennsy were known by number only.

Improvements

The Pennsy conducted tests to see which could be made to burn more efficiently, coal or wood, and the Pennsy steam running stock was 100 percent coal burning by 1864. During the coal/wood burning tests, the use of firebrick arch in loco fireboxes was shown to increase energy and efficiency, and from that time, it became standard equipment on steam locomotives throughout the Pennsy saga. The Pennsy also introduced the use of cast-iron drivers fitted with wrought-iron tires for use on most of its passenger locos. Freight locos still got the cast-iron driver chilled (hardened) tread treatment, however.

The swing bolster four wheel truck was another important innovation, as it improved on the older form of truck by dint of its side-to-side mobility; it actually 'guided' the loco around curves (the older truck was capable of swiveling, but could not deviate from the center line of the locomotive; the new truck 'swung' and actually followed the contours of the rails). Loco frames were getting longer— the swing bolster truck enabled

these larger locomotive designs to practically navigate existing trackage.

Braking Systems

Brakes were a crucial item, of course, and their development necessarily paralleled the ability of locomotives to run at higher speeds. The first brakes were discrete units, operated by crewmen assigned to work the hand wheel on each car by which they were operated. Then came the Cramer spring brake. This was a strong spiral spring mechanism which was wound tight at the beginning of each leg of a rail trip. From the mechanisms on each car, a cord ran to the engineer's station on the locomotive. When it was time to stop, the engineer pulled the cord, activating the brake on each car. It was then time to 'wind the brakes' again.

In 1855, the Loughridge chain brake improved on this somewhat. This system was a series of rods and chains connecting the brake shoes on each car to a small friction wheel, located behind the rearmost driving wheels of the locomotive. When braking time came, the engineer pulled a lever in his cabin which forced the friction wheel against the driver wheel, thus tightening the brake 'chain' throughout the train, and activating the brakes on each car.

In 1869, George Westinghouse developed his first air brake. This was a system whereby an air cylinder mounted on the engine was activated by the engineer to send compressed air through a system of flexible tubes to brakes on cars throughout the train. This resulted in vastly more responsive braking action. The drawback of this system was that the air reached car brakes *in succession;* the nearest cars to the engine braked first, then the next and so on, which again limited the allowable length of trains, and of course affected running speed. Also, if air pressure were lost, either by system failure or by a leak, the train had no brakes.

In 1873, Westinghouse improved his system with the 'Plain Automatic' air brake system. Each car was fitted with an auxiliary reservoir which was filled with air at train-line pressure when the train initially 'pumped up' its system. When train-line pressure was reduced for any reason, a valve device on the car auxiliaries released air from the auxiliaries into the brake cylinders, thus applying the brakes. The greater the reduction, the greater the brake shoe pressure—the valve was held shut by train-line brake pressure. This allowed the more nearly uniform applying of braking power throughout the train, and enabled the Pennsy (and other roads) to increase train lengths and run trains faster, as the Westinghouse 'Plain Automatic' air braking system proved a

safety success: if the brakes failed, they failed in being *locked on*— any rupture in a line would automatically lock the brakes up. This was the basis on which all modern air braking systems for trains have been designed.

All passenger locomotives on the Pennsy were equipped with automatic air brakes by 1 July 1879, and the Pennsy was the first railroad to adopt them as standard.

Standardization

On 16 November 1867, Alexander Cassatt became the Pennsy's Master of Machinery, and it was by his sugges-tion that the Westinghouse brakes be tried and adopted. Also by his tireless enthusiasm for a mechanically 'tight ship' the Pennsy embarked on its first program of locomotive standardization.

In the standardization program, eight classifications of needed motive power were set up for three main areas of service—freight, passenger and switching. In these eight classes, interchangeable parts and equipment were used as far as possible, and furthermore, the en-gines were designed specifically with their assigned usage in mind— to be built at the Altoona shops, or by locomotive contractors such as Baldwin. These locos saw Pennsy service for the first time between 1868 and 1872. By 1873, out of 916 locos in use, some 373 were

'standardized' locos, and they performed well. By 1876, more than half of the Pennsy's motive power was standardized.

This system used classification codes based on the first eight letters of the alphabet; in 1895, classifications were assigned a letter denoting wheel arrangement, which letter was followed by a number denoting a particular variation in that class (and sometimes this number was followed by another letter in a further attempt to pinpoint the variation—as in the E6s Atlantic passenger locomotive).

Originally, Class A engines were light passenger locos, B for passenger mountain helpers, C for passenger & fast freight trains; D locos were general service freight trains, E locos saw heavy mountain freight service; F engines were switchers with saddle tanks; G engines were used for light passenger service on branches and H engines were switchers with separate tenders. The Class C passenger locos were used far more than any other, and they were capable of making long non-stop runs by their use of *track tanks*—an important Pennsy innovation which allowed locomotives to literally scoop water into their tender tanks from long troughs situated between the rails. This enabled locos to take on water

Below: The 4–6–2 K4 Pacific, Pennsy's premier heavy passenger engine, averaged speeds of 70 mph and over. Pennsy steamers saved time by scooping water on the run from the Pennsy's between-rails 'track tanks.' *Above left:* A 2–8–2 Mikado. *Above:* A huge 2–10–0 11.

while in motion, for a reduction of stopping time on a run.

More Improvements

Tractive force increased, for example, from the Class K heavy fast passenger loco of 1880—with tractive force for its 157,000 pound weight being 11,860 pounds—to the Class S1 passenger loco of 1940—with tractive force of 71,900 pounds for an overall weight with tender of 1,060,010 pounds. Freight locomotives showed even more impressive gains—in weight as well as tractive force: Class R(H3) freight locos of the 1880s weighed 190,000 pounds and had tractive forces of 22,850 pounds; the Class Q2 freight locos of the 1940s developed 99,860 pounds of tractive force with their innovative four-cylinder design, and could up this to 114,860 pounds with a special booster unit—the loco with tender weighing 1,053,100 pounds—and the largest articulated steam loco ever used on the Pennsy, the Class HC1, built at Altoona in 1919, weighed 603,500 pounds, and with its huge boiler, cranked out a whopping 135,000 pounds of tractive force.

On 10 April 1876, the first pooling of locos for better routing and train configuring efficiency was effected on the Pennsy, that step being a natural follow-on to standardization of mechanical stock—standardization of procedure.

A much-used configuration for freight engines was the 'Consolidation' type—a 2-8-0 rear cab configuration which placed eight-ninths of its entire weight upon the driving wheels. The installation in 25 *Consolidation*-type locos of the big, square, Belpaire firebox marked them as the first locomotives to have this feature. The Pennsy's Altoona shops had built these engines, and in 1889, the first passenger locos with the Belpaire firebox saw Pennsy service.

Heavier Power

In 1895 a new 4-4-0 passenger engine was built at Altoona for the Class L heavy passenger trade. This engine was the beginning of a new breed of passenger engines—heavier, at 135,000 pounds.

Heavy passenger express engines of the 4-6-0 configuration were built at the Pennsy's Fort Wayne shops in 1893. These engines had 68-inch drivers and were classed 'X,' which would later be translated in the new classification system to G3. Others of this type were built at Altoona, and these were followed by a Baldwin-built rendition of this design—the G4a—in 1900.

In 1892, as the need for heavier passenger power became evident, six 4-4-0s with 78-inch drivers were built at Altoona. These locos of Class P (D14) were joined by further modified locos of their general configuration in 1894, which would become the new Class D14a.

Heavier freight engines were becoming necessary, too. In 1895, the F1 and the F1a Mogul 2-6-0s were conceived, followed in 1898 by the first H5 2-8-0, which was too big to turn on the turntable at Altoona, so the engine was used as a helper engine on the steep grade there. The H5 could haul 643 tons maximum—an advance over the Mogul's considerable 433-ton capacity, which in turn improved on the standard Class R freight

Shown *above* at the huge Enola freight yard, this 2-10-0 Decapod developed 90,000 lbs of tractive force, and weighed 590,000 lbs. Note its big, square firebox. The complex rod system connecting the wheels is the 'valve gear,' which regulates wheel motion—forward and reverse.

engine's 383-ton capacity.

In 1901, H6 Consolidations were improved, their design altered with wide fireboxes—these engines were produced at the Baldwin works. Ten of these were experimental, using the Walshaerts reversing valve gear, which proved so easy to service that it soon saw general usage on Pennsy locos. In 1910, more freight power was needed, and the H8 was designed—larger than the H6, with 62-inch drivers. This engine type was followed by two further improved types, the H9s and the H10s, some of which had automatic stoking systems, which created employment worries for firemen of the time.

The Pennsy's passenger traffic was also increasing, due to the increasing hustle and bustle of the traffic-rich East coast. For several years, locos with the 4-4-2 wheel configuration had been proving themselves effective in express passenger work. These were known as Atlantics. In 1899, the Pennsy built three of them with 80-inch drivers at Altoona, for the Camden-Atlantic City run. They pretty well did their chores, developing tractive force in the neighborhood of 28,000 pounds and hauling 300-ton trains at 75mph with ease and depend-

ability. These were classified E1. They were followed by Classes E1a, E2 and E3, which had radial-stayed fireboxes; the later E2 and E3 models had Belpaire fireboxes.

Atlantics were to be the standard engine for fast passenger service over the next decade, yet increasing passenger traffic demanded an even heavier passenger engine than the first Atlantics— this provoked investigation into Pacific-type locomotives, which were 4-6-2s. One of these was ordered from the American Locomotive Company in 1906. This loco proved useful, and as a result, the Class K-2 engine of this type was designed at the Fort Wayne shops, and a large number of these engines were built at the Altoona shops in the years following 1910. One of these was the first Pennsy loco to use a steam superheater, which allowed more power to be generated per given boiler capacity— sort of a 'supercharger' for steam locos. This equipment proved so useful that it became standard equipment on all Pennsy locos by 1913. The K3s class— K2's with superheaters— got its start with 30 Baldwin-built locos that year. These locos developed 38,280 pounds of tractive force.

The Pennsy's Altoona shops were the pulsing steel heart of the Pennsy mechanical plant. Locomotives were designed, maintenanced and built there, as were bridges (modularly, for shipment elsewhere) and other aspects of Pennsy track equipment. Many other important aspects of Pennsy road gear depended on this historical plant. While other shops had sprung up in the Pennsy system, Altoona, by dint of its central location, and its historically central position, remained the most important Pennsy shop.

In 1904, a full locomotive testing plant was designed— and erected at the Louisiana Purchase Exhibition in St Louis as a Pennsy exhibit. When the Exposition was over, the shop was dismantled, moved to Altoona, and resurrected for real work there.

The plant had the capability of analyzing any locomotive, regardless of size, type or configuration. Its main facility was a 'locomotive treadmill' composed of steel wheels upon which the drivers of test locomotives rested. These steel wheels were adjustable in terms of the amount of drag they could manifest against the tractive effort of the locomotive. The drag was created by use of hydraulic brakes, which could be set to simulate the drag produced when pulling a heavy freight, or climbing a steep grade. In short, the Pennsy test plant could reproduce actual running conditions, thereby enabling Pennsy equipment engineers to test locomotives completely.

The year 1910 saw the development of the heaviest

Atlantic, the E6s, developing a tractive force of 31,275 pounds, which outran the K2 in a test of pulling of 15-car trains. In 1913, 80 of these huge 4–4–2 speedsters were built at Altoona, and were put to work on the heaviest passenger runs in the New York and New Jersey divisions. The K4s, developing a tractive force of 44,460 pounds, superseded the E6s as the Pennsy's standard passenger loco, however, and remained in that position until the early 1930s. Some sources say that the K4 was essentially more an improved E6s with an extra pair of drivers than any close relative of a K2. The K4 was the essential Pennsy passenger locomotive; memories of a K4 in glistening Brunswick green thundering past at the head of a long line of Tuscan red passenger cars evoke one word: 'Pennsy.' That same year saw the development of the L1s Mikado type freight loco, which was an extra-heavy 2–8–2, with perhaps 25 percent more tractive power than the H9s.

The 10 wheeler Class I1s was born in Altoona in 1916. This engine was to prove hugely successful, becoming, until the 1940s, the standard heavy freight engine on the Pennsy. Engines of this type had automatic stokers and feed water heaters. The Juniata shops built 475 more for the Pennsy.

Streamlining

Streamlining was coming to Pennsy passenger service through the services of Raymond Loewy, the famous designer who would make, among other things, the Studebaker automobile look so distinctive in the late 1940s and early-to-mid 1950s. This was a K4s passenger locomotive which was given an aerodynamic bullet-like appearance that was to become very popular among railroads in the 1930s. Loewy worked in collaboration with the Pennsy's Engineering Department, conducting extensive wind tunnel tests with clay models. Still other streamlining treatments were given the Pennsy's K4s passenger fleet, but the Loewy work on number 3768 set the standard.

Four Cylinders

The advent of truly huge locomotives came with the Altoona shops' building of the Class S1, a streamlined 6–8–6 four-cylinder loco with 84-inch driving wheels, of which only one was built. This million pound-plus locomotive, the first of the modern multi-cylinder locos, had a tractive force of 71,900 pounds, and was designed to haul 1200 tons at 100 miles per hour. This type of engine was known as a 'duplex,' with two sets of high-pressure cylinders powering two sets of drivers rigidly mounted in the frame.

World War II saw the development of several multi-cylinder types. Among those used on Pennsy lines were the 2–10–4 J1 Class, developing a maximum tractive force of 110,100 pounds, many examples of which were acquired for use in the Pennsy's freight business. With the advent of this engine, for the first time in many years, a Pennsy loco did not incorporate into its design

Looking as if it's literally leaping forward, the 4–4–4–4 Class T1 locomotive *above right* could haul the heaviest passenger trains at over 100 mph, but it came late in the age of steam. Boxed photos: Powerful at nearly any speed was the GG-1, the pride of passenger electrics.

the Belpaire firebox. This was because the engine was an adopted design. Due to wartime restrictions, it was expedient to adopt the C&O's Lima-built 2-10-4 for the Pennsy's urgently-needed super freight hauler.

The Q1 was another four cylinder locomotive, having a 4-6-4-4 wheel arrangement, and it was redesigned to render for service the Q2, which produced more power at speeds over 20mph than any other steam loco ever built, had a maximum tractive force of 114,860 pounds, and could pull a 125-car train at more than 50mph. This development was followed by the T1, which could haul the heaviest passenger trains at over 100mph. The T1 had an interesting streamlining job done on it; the boiler head was tapered into a wedge shape, while its 'cowcatcher' resembled a broad, flat chin—giving the loco the appearance of something leaping ahead, imperiously sweeping all before it.

The first steam turbine loco saw service on the Pennsy in 1944. This loco represented Class S2, and eliminated the outside driving apparatus of traditional steam power. With no pushrods, cylinders and etc, it was driven by steam pressure against turbine blades. Jointly designed by Baldwin, Westinghouse and Pennsy engineers, this loco was seen by many as an effort to avoid dieselization. The loco was not a particular success, though it did develop respectable tractive force of 65,000 pounds.

Electric and Diesels

When the work on the Pennsy's Hudson River tunnels was progressing, and the electrification of the underground lines was taking place, the type of electric loco to be used on the lines was not yet fully decided. There were few electrical locomotives in existence then. Several experimental locos were built cooperatively by Pennsy and Westinghouse engineers, and these were further upgraded to produce a 4-4-0 locomotive with side rods and a 2000hp electric motor. These locos, classed as DD-1, had a high center of gravity, were very easy, therefore, on trackage, and were used in back-to-back pairs; built at Altoona with Westinghouse components, they saw continuous service throughout the late forties.

The opening of Broad Street station in Philadelphia, and the extensive electrification which took place in that area, produced the usage of the 11,000 volt overhead electrical system, which was better suited to such an expansive network. By 1924, there were some 286 motor cars in use, and by the mid-1940s, motor and traction-increasing slug car equipment in use on those lines increased to 524 units. In 1924, Class L5 engines were designed—these had side rods, and two were DC engines for use on the New York lines, while one was an AC engine used in the Philadelphia area. New York required the building of 21 more L5's.

The most powerful electric single unit ever built was the experimental 2-8-8-2 FF-1 loco, a side rod type developing 140,000 pounds of tractive force. After its few years of service in the late teens of this century, the loco was scrapped.

Switchers were developed for both AC and DC. Pennsy electrification spread, so that by February of 1936, the *Congressional Limited* became the first train in regular electric service—behind the best of the electrics, the famed GG-1—between New York and Washington.

The GG-1 was planned concomitantly with another loco, 4-8-4 R-1 with rigid trucks. These engines were tested for Pennsy's extensive passenger service with the 4-4-4 O1, a New Haven Railroad 4-6-6-4 electric and a K4s Pacific from 1933-35. The articulated-truck GG-1 was chosen for the job, hauling mostly passengers,

through some locos of this type were regeared and joined the P5A's in freight service.

Fourteen GG-1s were built in by General Electric, and 125 were built by the Pennsy's Altoona shops. Designed by GE and the Pennsy, these 100mph locos developed 4800 horsepower, and as late as 1979, saw regular service, handling *Metroliner* trains with one locomotive. At 79 feet, six inches, and with its 4-6-6-4 wheel arrangement, the GG-1, with its famous Pennsy 'pinstripe' paint job, symbolized reliability and efficiency for several decades.

Other long-range electrical locos were the 4-4-4 O1 class of light passenger haulers, eight of which saw service in the mid-thirties; the P-5A, progeny of the abortive P5, a 4-6-4 developing 56,250 pounds and capable of 90mph, of which 89 were built (some with box cabs) in 1932-33. Most of these locos went into passenger service, though some were given freight service gearing.

Diesels

In 1929, the Pennsy developed and built three gasoline-fueled switchers, for use in the New York field of operations. These had 400hp internal combustion engines, and remained in service with the road through the mid-forties; since their construction, however, one of them has been converted to diesel.

The Pennsy's first purchase of a true diesel-electric switcher occurred in 1937, and as of 1947, a total of 263 diesel-electric switchers, ranging from the small A6b car unit to the comparatively large 1000hp NW2 eight-wheel units— the familiar, if now rapidly disappearing, large-windowed, long-nosed units with the cab's door opening to the engine's rear.

The Pennsy initially, in 1945, bought an EMD (General Motors' Electro-Motive Division) two-unit,

4000hp diesel locomotive. This was to be a test bed for future purchases of this sort of power. A third unit was added to the engine, boosting its horsepower rating to 6000.

This spelled the end for the age of steam; as of 1 October 1947, 77 EMD diesels were on order for freight and passenger service. Baldwin also built switchers and passenger engines for the Pennsy. That firm, which had cooperated with and served the Pennsy's motor plant planning so well under the guidance of its founder Matthias Baldwin, and his successor at the helm, Samuel M Vauclain, would soon fade from the scene, losing money in such projects as steam turbine locomotives, and unable to build diesels that were quite as competitive as those produced by General Electric and Electro-Motive.

Diesels were hardy, and like the famed C-47 flying boxcar, would 'fly with a wing shot off and a tail missing.' They also used cheap fuel. Baldwin, that premier steam loco builder, was on its way out.

Baldwin produced several diesel models for the Pennsy, including the Baldwin-Westinghouse 0-4-4-0 switcher, which came in capacities ranging from 800hp to 1200hp. Besides these, several road diesels— including the famous 'shark nose' diesels— were turned out for the Pennsy.

During the war, Baldwin built a 'babyface' high windshield road diesel— with an articulated 4-8-8-4 running gear arrangement similar to that used on electric locomotives, and in 1947, the Pennsy bought 24

Shown *opposite* is a powerful L5 electric traction locomotive heading a train of mail cars at Manhattan Transfer in 1928. Note the electric third rail on this side of the engine. Diesel and electric wheel arrangements have a modern nomenclature all their own, but for the sake of simplicity, this text uses the same system— 4-8-4, etc— for all types. Riding the Pennsy four-track with a catenary system is the P-5A passenger engine *below*, which was photographed in 1933.

of these units, using them back to back for an effective force of 12 loco twins comprising 6000hp each.

The Pennsy also bought numerous shark nose models from Baldwin, these having an A (diesel) B ('slug,' or traction unit) working combination. Both A and B units were 4–4s, with all axles being driven by four Westinghouse traction motors. Generating engines for these units were single 1600hp eight cylinder diesels.

EMD F-3 and F-7 AB units were much in evidence on the Pennsy's lines, being 1500hp AB units. The engineer's vision was hampered by the diesel's high nose, and thus these were strictly road engines, unsuitable for yard work.

The following years saw an increasing use of a variety of diesels in all capacities by the Pennsy. Thousands of steam locos were scrapped, until, by the end of Pennsy's own line, there were no steam trains in use by the road. Since I have been unable to locate a comprehensive listing of engine types that were used on the Pennsy, the following is a 'second best' overview of some engines that would extend into the future to the inception of Conrail.

The Alco RS-3 saw service on lines that would become part of the Conrail network. It was a breakthrough with its cab placed such that engineers could actually see the road ahead, making for a more versatile locomotive, and for more road safety. This was a 1600hp 12 cylinder road switcher, designed to operate, with a few exceptions, 'long end first.'

Above: The great GG-1, capable of hauling long passenger trains at speeds in excess of 100 mph, served the various Pennsy permutations from the 1930s into the present decade, and is only now being threatened with retirement. *Below right:* A later model Pennsy passenger electric. Diesel mania was the big news in the late 1940s: a Pennsy favorite was the Baldwin shark nose model—an example of which is shown *at right* in construction for the Pennsy at the Baldwin shops.

The EMD GP-30's low nose and angular lines were part of a design scheme that set the cab far forward, for excellent visibility. The appearance of such engines as this marked the beginnings of an era in which improved electronics and features such as turbocharging would result in higher hp ratings for locos. This early sixties loco was a turbocharged 16 cylinder, 2250hp road switcher, at least some units of which were upgraded to higher horsepower when Conrail inherited the Penn Central.

The early seventies saw the use on future Conrail roads of the EMD SD-45. This is a 3600 horsepower 20 cylinder loco with 6–6 wheel arrangement. The 1970s generally marked the age of modularized loco electronics, such as are found on the General Electric U23-B 2300hp road switcher.

There were and are, of course, many more types of locomotives in use on the Pennsy and its progeny than are explicated in these pages. As previously stated, the lack of immediate specifics limits the selection here. For those more interested in modern motive power in the United States, Kalmbach Publishing Company offers some very fine reference books on the subject.

THE CASSATT YEARS

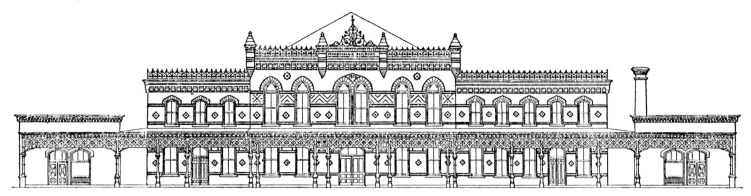

A Rates Remedy

During his brief but active retirement, Cassatt had studied the rationale behind, and the effects of, the ruthless rate wars that had destroyed so many railroads—not to mention the loss of respect and trust, for and in railroads, by the public and by legislators everywhere in the United States.

Cassatt had a plan ready to remedy this situation, which he enacted upon his accession to the Pennsy presidency on 9 June 1899.

The pooling system was quashed by the Interstate Commerce Commission Act of 1887. Though this new act uncompromisingly outlawed pooling, it proposed no substitute method of rates control, and gave the newly-formed commission no power to actually enforce fair rates; the ICC was a watchdog on a two-inch chain.

Large shippers such as Carnegie Steel were free to play one railroad against another to obtain exactly the shipping rates desired—at the expense of the railroads, of course—and at the expense of their smaller competitors, who hadn't the tonnage to manipulate rates and therefore payed higher rates than the larger firms did.

Cassatt's plan revolved around his belief that the weaker rail lines were responsible for the wild fluctuations in freight rates, as these roads were naturally desperate for business at any price. The solution, of course, was to buy into these roads and thus control them.

Previous pages: A big Pacific heads a Pennsy flyer on the Schuylkill River bridge in 1911. *Above:* Old West Philadelphia Station, built in 1875, was replaced with a newer, grander edifice in the Cassatt era.

Enlisting the aid of the likewise rates-besieged New York Central, the Pennsy and the NYC purchased more than 40 percent in interest in the stock of the Chesapeake & Ohio, which carried large volumes of bituminous coal. Shortly after this, the C&O's directorate was modified by the election of four directors from the NYC and four directors from the Pennsy. In 1901, the Pennsy acquired 30,000 additional shares of C&O stock.

From February to May of 1900, the Pennsy acquired 30 percent of the Norfolk & Western Railway's stock, then requested representation on the N&W's board, whereupon it was allowed to name six of the line's 11 directors. In late 1900, the Pennsy bought its holdings in the N&W up to 39 percent of that road's stock, or 338,300 shares. In November of 1899, Cassatt began buying stock in the B&O, and soon the Pennsy had 200,000 shares of B&O stock. By 1902, Pennsy purchases accounted for something over 40 percent of B&O stock. The Pennsy then elected its own fourth vice president, Leonor F Loree, to the presidency of the B&O.

These weaker roads had been made still more vulnerable by the Free Silver panic of 1896. The B&O had gone into receivership, for instance, and just previous to the Pennsy stock purchases had been reorganized with a smaller capital base.

At the same time the Pennsy was making its purchases, the NYC acquired control of the Lake Shore &

Michigan Southern; the Michigan Central (both of which were already Vanderbilt roads); the Cleveland, Cincinnati, Chicago & St Louis; and the Lake Erie & Western Railroad. Also, the Vanderbilt roads acquired some 20 percent stock interest in the Lehigh Valley RR Co, a heavy coal carrier.

The Reading was another weak link in the rates stabilization chain, having been reorganized in 1896. Offered to go 'halfies' in buying control of the road, the NYC demurred, as the Reading was a JP Morgan property. The Pennsy made its approach through the B&O, buying some 1,100,000 shares of leading stock: adding leverage to the Pennsy's control of the negotiations was the fact that the Reading was a close competitor for the B&O's New York routes. The NYC then 'tumbled to the deal,' and accepted the offered half interest through the offices of its Lake Shore & Michigan Southern Rail Road.

Cassatt recognized these purchases as temporary expedients to save a bad situation. Permanence was on his mind, though: if the Interstate Commerce Commission could be strengthened, then the rates could be regulated.

Cassatt led the fight for the Elkins Amendment to the ICC Act, which was made law in 1903. This and other legislation pursued by Cassatt added strength to the ICC and gave it powers of enforcement of its findings.

The Elkins Act made any deviation from published rates definite proof of rates descrimination, and provided heavy fines for grantors *and* receivers of rebates. Under the aegis of the Elkins Act, the ICC could take a suspected rates violator to court, and could obtain an injunction against that party upon proof of guilt.

Also in 1903, the Expediting Act gave precedence in federal courts to cases involving enforcement of the Antitrust Act and the Interstate Commerce Act.

In addition to these, the Hepburn Act was made law in 1906. This broadened the scope of the ICC. Now, express companies, sleeping car companies and rolling stock suppliers of all kinds, industrial railroads, private car lines, pipelines (other than oil or gas) and other transportation business fell within the control of the ICC.

Rates were stabilizing and rising to a reasonable, but not exploitative, level. The Pennsy therefore sold its holdings in the C&O, and most of its holdings in the B&O and the Norfolk & Western. (The Pennsy would later reacquire some of the N&W stock.)

The B&O itself and the Lake Shore retained most of the Reading holdings, but the Vanderbilt roads sold their Lehigh Valley interests.

The temporary rates relief was no longer needed when the ICC assumed its proper role, and the Pennsy and the NYC interests made healthy profits on the sales of their temporary holdings.

Improvements, Improvements, Improvements

It has been said that AJ Cassatt, during his tenure as President of the Pennsy, left his mark on almost every facet of the railroad. He actually rebuilt the line in part, and increased the capacity of the remainder. From 1899 to his death in 1906, a total of 1070 miles of new track-

Above: Alexander J Cassatt, whose many innovations and achievements brought the Pennsy to its peak of greatness. *Below left:* Magnificent Pennsylvania Station in Manhattan was truly a wonder of the world.

age had been added to the system, through acquisition and/or building of roads in New Jersey, the coal country and other points in Pennsylvania and Ohio.

Cassatt improved the mail lines system-wide, with extra trackage, grade and curve reductions and the elimination of grade crossings.

Under Cassatt, the main line was four-tracked from New York to Altoona, and almost all the way from Altoona to Pittsburgh, which track section was also relocated and/or regraded for faster running.

In New Jersey, the line from Camden to Atlantic City was double tracked and electrified by means of a 600 volt third rail using direct current; it remained so from 1906 to 1931.

Concerning 'Pennsy lines west,' the Pittsburgh, Fort Wayne & Chicago was double tracked entirely, and the Panhandle line was double tracked from Pittsburgh to Columbus. One third of the Indianapolis Division line west of Columbus got the same treatment.

On some roads, tracks were elevated to eliminate time consuming track crossings: track depressions did the same thing. Elevations were accomplished through Newark, New Brunswick, Camden, Chester, Wilmington and most of Philadelphia. In what had been Allegheny City (across the river from Pittsburgh), a costly system of elevations and depressions were effected; in Chicago, the Fort Wayne line's tracks were elevated from State Street in Englewood to the South Branch of the Chicago River.

Various terminal improvements were effected as well, including track elevation, new train sheds and work on a new terminal at Pittsburgh. In Philadelphia, the approaches to Broad Street station were upgraded and improved; a new passenger station went into operation at

Above: 'Sandhogs,'aka a tunnel crew, pose at the mouth of one of the Hudson River tunnels. The man with the white moustache is Charles Jacobs, supervisor of the Pennsy's Hudson River tunnels construction.

32nd and Main Streets in West Philadelphia (this was replaced by the 30th Street station in 1933); and Pennsy line tracks approaching the station from the south, west and north were relocated farther apart, to reduce conflict between these incoming lines. This specific change resulted in the building of two new bridges across the Schuylkill to handle the new track positionings. Track improvements were made so that New York-Washington trains could pass through the city non-stop. Other grade separations and terminal improvements were made.

Freight cutoffs routed trains around all principal points of congestion on the main line, and all manner of improvements were made, for as Frank P Donovan Jr put it, 'It was the first decade of the 20th century and the Pennsylvania was being built bodily into a 20th century transportation machine.'

From 1899 to 1906, the Pennsy's total assets rose from $276 million to $594 million— an *increase* of 115 percent, and its investment in trackage and equipment increased by 146 percent. This growth was miraculous for an entity already 50 years old, and even more phenomenal is that this old Goliath of a road was handling one-fifth of the country's freight tonnage and one-sixth of its passengers.

Everything about the Cassatt era was big, including the stations and locomotives themselves (see Pennsy Locomotives). A new Union Station in Washington DC— which was planned by joint agreement (approved by a special Act passed in Congress) between the Philadelphia, Baltimore & Washington and the Baltimore & Ohio— was laid out, and when the monumental granite building was completed in 1908, it had 32 station tracks; 20 at station level and 12 below for trains from

the South. On the northern approach, five bridges bore trackage above the capital's streets; one of these bridges carried 30 tracks, and another, 27. The southern trains approached through a twin-tubed tunnel which was 4033 feet long. The station's waiting room, 220 feet long by 130 feet wide, was one of the largest in the country. Of the station's 632 foot by 210 foot bulk, the concourse, with a volume of 97,500 square feet, was for years 'the largest room under one roof in the world.'

Tunnels to New York

Alexander Cassatt was a man who accomplished great things despite great obstacles. He loved his family, keeping up an active life with relatives despite the intensities of railroading. His interests were invariably serious: he was known as 'one of the two or three leading patrons of American turf,' for his interest in breeding and racing horses; and for 19 years he was road supervisor of Lower Merion Township, near Philadelphia, out of his concern for better public roads.

The point at which the Pennsy would have to cross the river was almost a mile wide— at the time, a daunting bridge prospect. However, *tunnel* construction methods had improved. Cassatt had recognized what most Pennsy officials would not admit: New York City had stolen Philadelphia's crown as the nation's hub of trade, and the Pennsy could not afford to continue ferrying its cars across the river at the expense of its passengers.

On 12 December 1901, Cassatt—not usually a man to air his business intention publicly—announced the Pennsy's intent to build new facilities.

This project would tie together the Pennsy's holdings in New York, and the recently acquired Western New York & Pennsylvania line gave access to Rochester and Buffalo with its 585 miles of trackage. All in all, the Pennsy's 6032 miles of tracks east of Pittsburgh and 5048 miles west of Pittsburgh were a challenge to all competitors. Cassatt proposed that his line's 100 million yearly passengers be transported by rail directly to the Big Apple.

The plan had actually been born in 1871, when the United Railroads of New Jersey came into the Pennsy fold. The crossing of the Hudson at its mouth was an unprecedented task, and the Panic of 1873 shelved plans for such a crossing.

By 1884, plans were under consideration to build a Hudson River bridge twice the length of the Brooklyn Bridge—this was to be a joint project involving several railroads terminating on the river's western shore. The Panic of 1893 interfered.

Such a bridge could only receive a charter if it were to involve *several* railroads, and when the Pennsy found itself standing alone with the bridge idea at the turn of the century, alternate means seemed to be the answer. The earliest proposed substitute for the passenger ferries had, in fact, been a tunnel under the Hudson. Electricity, which would play a big part in the success of the Cassatt administration scheme, had not been sufficiently developed to provide smokeless power for the trains, and Pennsy officials were against running steam locos in submarine tubes.

Haskin's Tunnel

Despite these drawbacks, DeWitt Haskin organized the Hudson River Tunnel Company in 1874. Haskin's tunnel would run from 15th Street in Jersey City and would surface in Manhattan. It was to include a Manhattan terminal building for all the railroads blockaded by the Hudson.

The tunnel's route paralleled that of the Lackawanna Railroad's Christopher Street ferry, and that railroad successfully blocked the project with an injunction until 1880.

Haskin's experience with tunneling involved hard rock mining in the West. He was not well prepared to cope with the Hudson's soft riverbed. The men who worked in the tunnel descended in caissons—water tight boxes—and then entered air locks where they waited until 12 pounds of air pressure was developed in the tunnel. Sometimes, on the return to the surface, the men experienced excruciating pain, nausea, illness—sometimes they died of this mysterious malady which was known then as the 'caisson disease,' and which we call today 'the bends,' so named for the agonizing contortions its sufferers endure. The 'disease' was the result of pressurized air, which produced excess nitrogen in the workers' bloodstreams. If one went from pressurized air to normal air too quickly, the nitrogen formed bubbles in the bloodstream, causing intense pain and sometimes death.

Another danger was nascent in Haskin's very ignorance. The tunnel's sides had to be solid enough to hold the pressure in. If the pressure escaped, there was a 'blowout,' in which men and equipment were literally spewed out the leak.

On the morning of 21 July 1880, assistant engineer Pete Woodland and his men found the tunnel to be very 'soft.' Woodland saw a trickle of water, sounded the alarm, ran to the air lock and held the door open for his men. Eight men had rushed into the airlock when the river burst full force into the tunnel. Woodland slammed the door, saving the men in the lock from the death that he and 19 other of their fellows suffered in that tragedy. The Haskins project itself eventually collapsed in 1891.

Pennsy Tunnels

In 1892, spurred by Long Island Railway President Austin Corbin's studies in rapid transit lines, Pennsy president Roberts sent his assistant, Samuel Rea, to London to study the operation of the London 'tubes.'

Rea returned from London, and prepared a lengthy report on the possibilities of 'crashing' Manhattan other than by ferry. Corbin championed a tunnel from Jersey City to Manhattan near the Battery, and then across the East River to Atlantic Avenue in Brooklyn.

A second proposal featured a rail line from Rahway, New Jersey across Staten Island and into a 3 1/2-mile tunnel under the Narrows to Brooklyn, then back across the Narrows to a terminus on Madison Avenue in Manhattan; this plan was deemed to be overcomplicated.

The third plan was for a high-level bridge across the river which would include a station at Sixth Avenue from whence a connection would be made, via a tunnel under 42nd Street, with the Long Island Railroad. This bridge would have 14 tracks on two levels, 10 for steam trains and four for rapid transit.

Even though the eminent engineer Gustav Lindenthal was the designer of the bridge concept, the Panic of 1893 frightened the Pennsy's prospective partners away from the project.

In 1901, Samuel Rea suggested to Alexander Cassatt that he attend the opening of the Extension of the Orleans Railway in Paris: the system's electric locomotives and tunnel system convinced Cassatt that now was the time to tunnel under the Hudson.

Cassatt's main concerns were safety (the Haskin disaster being a grim lesson), durability of construction and proper accommodation of rail traffic. A feasibility study was conducted by the Pennsy's hand-picked board of eminent engineers. The chairman of the board was Colonel Charles W Raymond of the US Army's Corps of Engineers; under him were Gustav Lindenthal, with 15 years of Pennsy engineering experience; Charles Jacobs, the English tunnel expert; Alfred Noble, an expert in bridge and canal construction, previously appointed by President McKinley to the Isthmian Canal Commission; and William H Brown, chief engineer of the Pennsylvania Railroad. George Gibbs, an expert in electric traction locos, was added to the board in 1902.

This board reported to Rea, now a vice president under Cassatt. The Manhattan terminal was to be a *through* terminal—unusual in that most large city terminals tended to be end terminals. The station was to be situated over the railroad tunnel, which would dive from New Jersey under the Hudson, straight across

Manhattan Island, under the East River into Long Island to the Sunnyside Yards complex, and thence via a connecting line across the western tip of Long Island and across a bridge above the treacherous waters of the Hell Gate channel to the tracks of the Pennsy subsidiary New Haven Railroad to provide a through line all the way up the Atlantic Coast!

The line was brought across New Jersey's Hackensack Meadow, then over a high landfill to Bergen Hill, whose two single track tunnels burrowed under the Hudson, meeting the station in Manhattan at 10th Avenue between 31st and 33rd Streets; the tracks remained under street level and increased from two to 21 as they fed into the station. The Long Island tracks proceeded in four single track tunnels, from Long Island City to dive below the East River at the Sunnyside yards, on into Manhattan where they connected with the trackage beneath the station.

Cassatt apportioned the work into four divisions: William Brown would supervise the Meadows Division, which encompassed the line from Manhattan Transfer—the station at Harrison, New Jersey, where incoming trains switched from steam locos to electric traction locos for the tunnel journey (and vice versa outgoing)—to the tunnel portals at the mouth of the Hudson.

The North River Division ran from Bergen Hill, under the river, to 10th Avenue in Manhattan, and was under the supervision of Charles Jacobs. The trackage from Seventh Avenue, under the East River, to the Long Island line was the east river division—under Alfred Noble, who also oversaw the 206-acre maintenance and equipment cleaning facility called Sunnyside Yard.

George Gibbs was in charge of the Electric Traction and Station Construction Division, which saw to the electrification of the necessary trackage, and also would build the steel-structural shell for the mammoth new station.

Both of the Hudson tubes were completely dug, but were yet to be lined by 1906. By the spring of 1909, the work was so far along that the board of engineers was dissolved. On 8 September 1910, the station was serving the Long Island's trains; November 27 of that year saw the completion of the tubes-and-station project, with Pennsy trains in full service.

The four-track, 1000 foot-long Hell Gate bridge and its attendant lines opened on 1 April 1917.

The tunnels under the Hudson were first contracted in 1904. The work was to be done by the 'shield method': the shield was a giant cylinder with nine doors in it through which the mud, rock and debris of the riverbed was passed. This shield was the vanguard for a series of concentric rings—which formed the lining of the tunnel—that the workers constructed by bolting two 1/2-footlong flanged cast iron plates together. The shield protected the work already done in case of a blowout of the tunnel section being bored.

The riverbed was soft, but the traprock in areas such as Bergen Hill was very hard, and here the work proceeded at the pace of six feet per day, more or less.

Huge air compressors pumped pressure into the tunnels to prevent cave-in. This compression, of course, created the danger of the bends. Cassatt—remembering the disaster of 1880, and taking heed of Washington Roebling's crippling by the bends while he was working on the Brooklyn Bridge—took extensive measures to protect his workers.

Heated lockers were designed to dry the men's work clothes each day, so that they wouldn't have to work in wet clothing; hot and cold baths were ready for the men when they ended their shifts; hot coffee (thought to be an antidote to compression) was in plenteous supply; air locks inside the tunnels were complemented by 'hospital' locks at the surface (in case a man showed signs of the bends) and these hospital locks were equipped with a full array of medical equipment, plus a depressurized compartment from which a doctor could tend a sick man.

Troubles

Accidents did, however, occur. On 20 June 1906, a blowout in an East River tunnel killed two men and injured two others. Previous to this, the contractors doing the actual construction had reported several deaths due to the bends. A coroner's jury severely censured the contractors for carelessness. Samuel Rea defended the contractors in the press, pleading the extreme complexity of their task.

Cassatt, who had a heart ailment which had been deemed serious as early as 1894, was very upset by the deaths, and was himself trying to recuperate from the death of his favorite daughter Katherine—newly married, she died on 11 April 1905 from hyperthyroid complications.

In late June 1906, Cassatt took a much-needed vacation with his family. He contracted whooping cough, which was a dreaded disease at the time. His children soon came down with it, and the ailing Cassatt spent his own sick time tending to them.

On September 12, several 'sandhogs'—the tunnel workers' popular appellation—from the New York end of a Hudson tube passed cigars to their New Jersey colleagues through a small hole at the rim of their respective shields: the shields had met! Now the job of cement-lining, bracing and finishing lay ahead; the conclusion of which we have already told. The second Hudson tube punched through on October 9.

On December 3, a premature explosion in one of the East River tubes cost the lives of five men.

Interstate Commerce Commission investigations which showed that trusted Pennsy officials had accepted graft combined with these more recent tube deaths to weigh the ailing Alexander Cassatt down even more: he had had to fight against graft in his struggle to get the permits to build his station in New York. By early December, Cassatt stopped going to his office; for the first time, the family Christmas dinner was canceled; and on 28 December 1906, Alexander Cassatt, age 67, died.

A New Era

James McCrea followed Cassatt into the Pennsy presidency. The year 1907 marked the apex of a curve of rapid growth that had begun in 1896.

Perhaps the downward economic trend which began at this time was sparked by continued public distrust of the railroads. The Roosevelt administration's anti-trust

Above: Looking west from under the station, we see the Hudson River tunnel portals in this 1937 photo. Note the extensive overhead electrical catenary system for feeding lots of juice to hungry Pennsy electrics— the type of motive power that made the tunnels possible.

policies added to this air of railroad watchdogging, and in any event, money was not as 'loose' as it had been in the decade up till then.

McCrea's administration was one of mild improvements made at various points in the Pennsy system, new acquisitions totaling 666 miles, and of following through on the monumental Cassatt projects.

The Pennsy Versus the Aldermen

Cassatt made certain preparations for building his station. He knew of the standing tradition among the aldermen of New York— that if anything were to be done in their precincts, the doer would have to pay and pay. Cassatt hated that sort of thing— not out of chintziness, simply out of hatred for kickbacks, bribes and all that they stood for. In 1901, Cassatt quietly enlisted the aid of the honest mayor of New York City, Seth Low.

Low made Cassatt promise that he would be entirely above board, for any attempts to go 'on the sly' would be made immediate fodder for the aldermen's usual practice of creating a public outcry until their demands were met. Low conducted a public meeting on the steps of city hall between the aldermen and the city's Rapid Transit Commission; together, they worked out a compromise franchise bill, but the aldermen held negotiations up for weeks— they wanted their money! Cassatt refused to pay the $300,000 that they demanded.

Cassatt held firm, and for once, the public and the newspapers allied themselves with a major corpora-

tion— they came to Cassatt's aid; the mayor assured the newspaper editors that Cassatt and the Pennsy were sincere in their offer to do a great service for New York City by building a massive transit terminal on the verge of Hell's Kitchen— couldn't it be possible that businesses would be attracted there?

Cassatt won the franchise in January 1902. The New York State Legislature had already agreed to amend the Rapid Transit Act to allow the Pennsy to close streets and to raze buildings— within proper channels— in order to build the new station and tunnels complex.

A Colossal Design

On 24 April 1902, Cassatt interviewed Charles F McKim, the senior partner of the architectural firm of McKim, Mead and White, and accepted his bid of $250,000 to design and oversee construction of the $50 million station. It was to be built between Seventh and Eighth avenues and 31st and 33rd streets.

Pennsylvania Station would be nearly twice as big as the Hamburg terminal, then the world's largest, and would be thrice the size of South Station in Boston, the largest in the United States. It would encompass six city blocks— far larger than a football field, or even two football fields! McKim's responsibilities as an architect

would be limited to the building 'above the waiting room level,' as Cassatt's own engineers would set the retaining walls and foundations, and would basically set up the station's nitty-gritty theater of operations—the track bed and so on.

Cassatt's old acquaintance George Westinghouse was called in to do the station wiring, the lighting for the tunnels, and the heating and ventilation for passenger train service. Samuel Rea was made the liaison between Westinghouse, Mckim and the various contractors who would eventually do the work, and Cassatt had the final say in any dispute that arose.

Thirty-Second Street between 7th and 10th looked, as one account put it, like the Panama Canal under construction. Twenty-eight acres of ground had been cleared, over 500 buildings had been purchased and demolished; townhouses were bought and razed to make way for the tunnel construction. There were mishaps with the tunnels—the crews had to constantly be wary of bursting water mains and gas lines; sewer lines, of course, had to be avoided; building foundations had to be skirted. At one point, a charge of dynamite that had been misplaced exploded near the site of the station excavation, injuring nearly 20 bystanders, some of them severely. A coal cart sank into the street in front of the Waldorf Astoria hotel. All of this was born by New Yorkers with an amazing degree of calm—perhaps because the station excavation itself was taking on the air of an eighth wonder of the world.

The excavation went down 58 feet through granite-like gneiss; it stretched for two city blocks on either side of Eighth Avenue, which had been transformed into a land bridge closed to traffic. The Ninth Avenue elevated railway presented problems—its structure had to be reinforced from below to allow the excavation work to continue, and blasting was held up when trains passed over it. Altogether, the excavation was a sight beheld and marveled over by many New Yorkers, as it was a wonder, and the catch-phrase 'I can see down to China!' was born of it.

But it was nothing to the station that would rise from it, whose mighty trains would ply the incredible tunnel system to points up and down the coast, to the deep South, and to Chicago and all points between it and New York City, the queen city of the USA.

Down in the tunnels, men worked in the nerve-jangling noise and the unsettling clamminess of subterranean twilight; in the station 'hole,' men manipulated huge machines amid dust and seeming confusion to prepare the way for a building that partook of the famed Crystal Palace, in its airy traceries of iron and glass, and the Roman baths at Caracalla—which had been the mutual inspiration of both Charles McKim and Alexander Cassatt, who shared Continental tastes— both men had been struck by the monumental, yet elegant style of the ancient baths.

Like Alexander Cassatt, Charles McKim never saw the completion of the magnificent building he had begotten. Feeling tired, he went to his summer retreat on Long Is-

land for a rest. His long-time partner Stanford White had shortly before been murdered. That, and the immense work on the station, took its toll on the aging McKim. On 14 September 1909, Charles McKim died with his daughter at his side. Like so many men of those exciting and often heartbreaking times, he had died of heart failure.

The station was finished in 1910; 15 million bricks, 27,000 tons of steel and 150,000 cubic yards of concrete were wed to 550,000 cubic feet of Milford pink granite which had been transported in 1140 freight cars from the quarries of Massachusetts. The granite was for 'ornamentation.'

The station's exterior design was a Roman Doric colonnade, with a low attic broken by pavilions to indicate each of the four principal doorways. Entablatures were set above the four entrances, and 60 feet above the sidewalk, on each facade, was a granite wreath-encircled, seven foot-wide clock, which was flanked by sets of classically sculpted maidens who were themselves flanked by sculptor Adolph Weinman's eagles.

Beyond the Seventh Avenue vestibule, passengers arriving by foot (carriages were received at porticoed carriageways, modeled after the Brandenburg Gate, at either end of the Seventh Avenue entrance), entered the 'arcade,' illuminated from far above by lunette windows which were set close to the vaulted ceiling—and their lights shown down in intersecting rays that glowed on the marble floor. The arcade was a thoroughfare lined with shops for passenger convenience. The shops were like little cages made of metal, separated by honey-colored travertine marble.

The 'loggia' awaited passengers at the end of the arcade. This colonnaded vestibule was an approach to the main waiting room. Facing south from the loggia was a formal dining room and cafe, large enough to accommodate 500 people; on the north side of the station, on the other side of the loggia, was a lunchroom and coffee shop, also large, and comprising what must have been— and would still be— remarkably elegant accommodations for such an informal eatery. Also at this point of expectation in one's entrance to the station were two niches, set at the top of the grand staircase, which was carved of Italian marble. In one of these niches, overlooking the vastness of the main waiting room, was a statue of Alexander Cassatt. The other niche awaited—until 1930, to be exact—the statue of Cassatt's good lieutenant, Samuel Rea.

The waiting room itself was modeled after the tepidarium of the Baths at Caracalla. Fashioned almost entirely of the warmly glowing travertine, the waiting room was 150 feet high, with huge lunette windows 65 feet across at their bases, tucked up close to the coffered ceilings. The room was in effect a huge clerestory, with the light from the windows forming ever-changing patterns on the scene below. Beneath the windows, huge topographical maps in shades of blue and tan represented the Pennsylvania Railroad's territory—these had been painted by the artist Jules Guerin. Ticket and telegraph offices, also made of marble, appeared to coalesce with the walls themselves, as if carved from a single stone. Marble pedestals upholding iron candelabra were the sole source of artificial light in the huge room.

At left: Pennsylvania Station's main waiting room, facing one of the two side entrances—beyond the far doors of this entrance was a bridge over a carriageway, leading to 31st Street. To the right is the main staircase. The main columns here were six stories high. In true Roman style, there were no seats in this vast waiting room.

Passengers crossing the great room might have observed stairways flanking them to the right and the left—these marked the 31st and 33rd Street entrances. They were flanked by six Ionic columns, led to stone bridges over the carriageways, and thence, to the outside world. At the west end of the room were two subsidiary waiting rooms, one for men—which was connected to a lavatory, a changing room and a barber shop; and one for women—which led to a lavatory, which in turn was approached through a 'retiring' room.

Beyond this, the center and 'heart' of the entire station, lay the grand concourse, a regal vestibule to the tracks 400 feet long, arched over by a glass and steel dome that at once suggested might and power—and a delicate airiness. It was a room of extreme contrasts, of white and black and shadows, a place where the conductor's voice rang out, the last goodbye was said, the delighted hello beckoned. This was a place of departures and of homecomings—a place of vitality and memory. It had been modeled after the great train sheds of Europe, places where human interactions twined with the memories of centuries of culture, places where art and life had become inextricably fused.

The intense and elegant shadow play of the gigantic station penetrated hearts from all over the world in its

Above and above right: Opposing views of the main concourse. With its flights of structural steel and glass, it was the dramatic stage for countless homecomings and departures—in 1945 alone, this airy yet substantial room would host over 109 million people. The wrought iron stairways led down to the track platforms. *At right:* The station's spacious lunch counter embodied a formality that would have given any snack refulgence. Note the chandeliers and large, elegant windows.

50-odd years of existence. Changes were made here and there toward the end of its days, but the sense that some of the most important moments of many lives were played out here hung in its air. It was that very special something that a place becomes when wives say goodbye to husbands going off to war, and when the ticket in your hand means the start of a new life in another town, another country, maybe even another time—as place and history become one. World War I, World War II, the Great Depression, the Roaring Twenties—all the flappers and soldiers and gangsters and families and sailors, secretaries, shysters, congressmen, farmers, cops, poets and dishwashers—the millions who would pass through this place would leave part of their lives here—even if just as an echo or a feeling. It was a place designed for the upliftment of one and all, and to underscore the greatness of the one and only Pennsylvania Railroad; it was almost anything you wanted it to be—it was Pennsy Station.

WORLD WAR I AND THE TWENTIES

Sam Rea

Samuel Rea, fresh from a job well done on the Manhattan tunnels and station project, was elected to the Pennsy presidency on 13 November 1912, and assumed his office on 1 January 1913.

Born on 21 September 1855, Rea had worked his way up through the Pennsy hierarchy—from chainman to construction engineer to head of all Pennsy construction work, and finally to the vice-presidency under Mr McRea.

The Hell Gate Bridge Project

One of the signal events of his administration was the construction of the Hell Gate Bridge project. The tracks were to run from Port Morris (connecting with the New Haven Railroad via its Harlem & Port Chester branch) to Fresh Pond junction, and finally to Bay Ridge connecting with Long Island's main line, and from there to the Pennsy water terminal at Greenville. Generally, the line would cross the East River and Hell Gate using Randall's and Ward's Islands as stepping stones.

Because of the angle of approach from Ward's Island, only an arch-style bridge was feasible. The turbulence of the Hell Gate channel was such that halves of the arch would have to be built out from piers on either side of the channel, with no bracing to support them from beneath—backstays had to be used to suspend the curved sections until they were fused together into one arch at the middle. Hell Gate Bridge was the largest arch bridge attempted at that time, carrying four railroad tracks over its 1000-foot length.

Auxiliary bridges in this system included a four-span, 1200 foot-long bridge between Randall's Island to the New York mainland over the Bronx Kill.

The entire line across Long Island was elevated as well. The Hell Gate Bridge line was opened for passenger service on 1 April 1917. The project was finished in December of 1917, and the passenger lines were electrified in early 1918.

Tracks to Detroit

In 1917, the Pennsy formed a company to build a line into the thriving, potentially lucrative city of Detroit. Trackage and terminal agreements were made, by way of establishing connecting lines, with the Pere Marquette and the Wabash. The plan was to run Pennsy trains from Toledo to the Ohio-Michigan border, where they would connect with the Pere Marquette to Carleton, thence over a 20 mile connecting track (built entirely new by the Pennsy) to the River Rouge, where connection to the Wabash would be made, thence to jointly-owned Wabash and Pere Marquette tracks, then to a connection with tracks under usage agreement with the Fort Street Union Depot Company, owners of a depot in Detroit where the Pennsy would enter the city.

World War I interrupted these plans, but passenger service was inaugurated by 1920, and all work on the line was completed in 1923.

Various other additions and improvements were carried out under Mr Rea, including the simplification of the Pennsy's corporate structure, which entailed dissolving the Pennsy's holding company, known as the Pennsylvania Company, as well as consolidations of numerous of the Pennsy's smaller branch lines, into larger, more conveniently managed units.

The War

The freight problem in World War I has been discussed elsewhere in this text. The bottlenecks inherent in the Railroads' War Board priorities system enjambed the Pennsy's Pittsburgh operations to the point that an Operating Committee was sent in November of 1917 to monitor such eastern railroad burdenage handling, and the committee almost immediately embargoed all freight shipments moving through Pittsburgh. The ICC was generally satisfied with the Railroads' War Board's performance, but on 5 December 1917, President Wilson issued a proclamation announcing government takeover of US railroads under the 1916 War Powers Act. The takeover was effective as of 28 December 1917.

Part of this takeover was a program of additions made to railroads specifically for wartime operation—a feature which would prove to be economic bad news for postwar rail operation budgets, in this and especially in World War II, as these 'improvements' were paid for by the railroads.

The government made various agreements with the different shop unions of the American Federation of Labor, a move that was to boost Pennsy employment by 20 percent and overall wages by 111 percent.

Return of Company Control

The Transportation Act of 1920 returned the railroads to the control of their owners on 1 March 1920, and extended federal compensation to 31 August 1920. This federal compensation helped to keep the Pennsy out of some financial trouble, but freight rates were not adequate to meet increasing employee wage demands.

An 'outlaw,' or unauthorized, switchmen's strike occurred in April of 1920, further compounding a difficult situation. Net railway operating income for the first four months of the Pennsy's fiscal 1920 was $11.9 million, compared to the averaged deficit for the same fiscal period of $21 million.

The year 1921 saw a serious economic downturn in the nation's freight business. By January, the Pennsy had 300,000 idle freight cars. Freight was down 23 percent from 1920, and passenger carriage was down 14 percent. The road's stock dividend had to be cut to four percent.

Certain operating principles had been in force since the government takeover of the railroads, and these expensive-to-implement procedures had been kept in force by the roads at the special request of the new Labor Board. Hearings were to be held to determine these procedures' actual merits.

Union Representation

The aforementioned hearings were held on 14 April 1921, and the wartime conditions were dissolved on 1 July of that year. However, the Labor Board also set up

Previous pages: An E2 4-4-2 Atlantic passenger engine. The original number 7002, an E3, hit 127.1 mph with the *Pennsylvania Special* in 1905. WWI: *Above,* a whistle stop; *at top,* the Liberty Bell on tour.

16 principles by which railroads were to negotiate wages and working conditions with their employees.

WW Atterbury, acting on the part of the Pennsy, agreed to these conditions, and the Labor Board was immediately notified of all arrangements that the Pennsy had made with its workers.

At the Altoona shops—the hub of the Pennsy's entire mechanical stock maintenance program—employees voted for fellow workers to represent them in labor negotiations. Everywhere else in the Pennsy system, the unions had convinced workers that organizations—ie, specific union chapters—should represent employees at negotiations. The shop crafts were incensed that Altoona had voted for individual representation, and went before the Labor Board with this grievance. The Labor Board struck down the negotiations between individuals and companies, upholding the union representation system.

Fearing that they were being set up on a charge of breaking the Labor Board's edict, Pennsy officials obtained a temporary injunction against the Labor Board from issuing a decision on the matter.

A year later, the injunction was declared null and void by the US Supreme Court—in a decision which also defined the powers of the Labor Board as merely persuasive, and not mandatory.

Railroads were hurting, and several roads went to the Labor Board requesting permission to reduce wages. The response was affirmative, and to smooth the process out a little, the Board told the unions that they would be held in contempt if they rebelled. Wages were rolled back to the 1920 levels.

The only strike to result from this was the shop-crafts workers strike, which occurred in mid-summer 1922, and was the first nationwide railroad strike in US history. The Pennsy, having stuck to its 'individuals' negotiation methods of the year before, fared reasonably well in the strike. By the end of July 1922, a new agreement had been reached with the Pennsy employees who had not struck, and by September, Pennsy shop employment was up to 91 percent of normal.

The Roaring Twenties

The years 1923 through 1929 saw a continuous increase in operating income, with expenses holding steady: the Pennsy was healthy again.

One bone of contention between railroads and the government was the stipulation of the Transportation Act of 1920 that was intended to deal with the almost traditional financial instability of the nation's railroads. Congress had determined that railroads were entitled to earn five and 1/2 percent on their value, and that any profit over that amount in a given year would be split 50/50, with half of such excess going to a contingency fund for each railroad's own lean years, and half going to a fund for the upkeep and maintenance of some of the nation's weaker railroads.

The ICC's Consolidation Plan

A long-term solution to the problem of unequal competition among railroads was sought by the Interstate Commerce Commission. The ICC's powers had increased to include a wide range of effectiveness. The ICC could regulate rates, approve or disapprove securities, oversee and approve or prevent construction of new lines, approve of the leasing of one rail carrier by another, and more.

Part of this consideration was a long-term study concerning the feasibility of consolidating smaller lines into large trunk lines, thereby reducing the number of the nation's ailing railroads to a relatively healthy few. This would hopefully level out the competition curve, as the fight then would be among comparative equals.

Since the Pennsy was the largest railroad in the world, having moved more freight along its 11,107 miles of track than any other (at its peak, the Pennsy moved 1/20th of the entire world's freight commerce!), the consolidation concept had little to offer the giant road.

But the idea was gaining ground, and the ICC's hiring of Dr William Zebina Ripley saw the inauguration of a series of consolidation proposals. Ripley planned that, among other great changes in the American railroad landscape, the Norfolk & Western would be disassociated from the Pennsy, and would be made the anchor of a new, consolidated, road; the Reading would become part of the B&O; the Lehigh would go to the Erie. The Ripley Plan's five eastern trunk lines would be the Pennsy, the NYC, the B&O, the Erie-Lehigh Valley and the Nickel Plate-Lackawanna.

The ICC enlarged and altered this plan, and subsequent plan hearings resulted in further plans, until, when all was said and done, some five different plans had been offered and considered, each with its own merits and drawbacks, and none had been agreed upon— either by the ICC or by the major trunk lines, whose approval was of course necessary. The major trunk lines gave up their negotiations in this area of consideration in 1925.

Big, fast 4–4–2 Atlantics such as those at *above right*— here hustling a vintage Pennsy express near Mount Joy, PA— were the Pennsy's thoroughbreds. *At right:* A diesel 'hotshot' freight at Bird in Hand, PA.

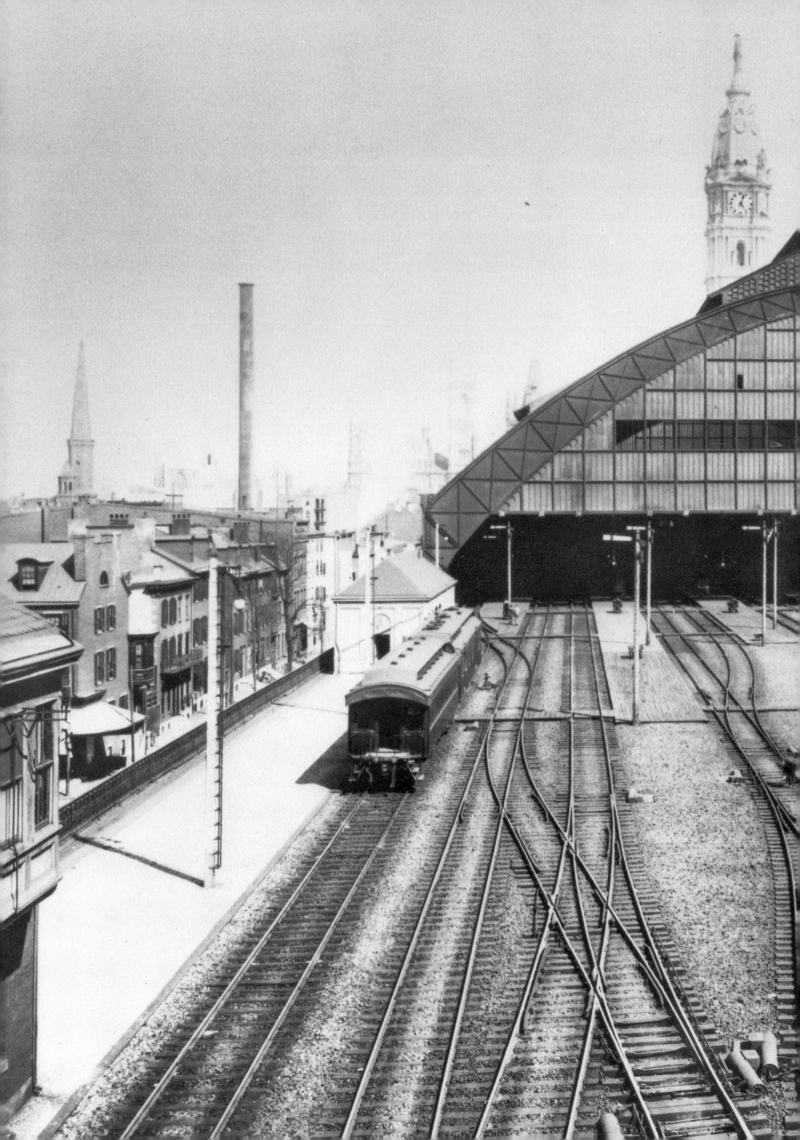

BOOM AND BUST AND WAR AGAIN

The Late Twenties

William Wallace Atterbury succeeded Samuel Rea on 1 October 1925. Atterbury, like many Pennsy presidents, had worked his way up in the company. During World War I, while holding the Pennsy post of vice president in charge of operations, Atterbury was chosen, after a nationwide request made by the war department for the 'ablest man in the country,' to run the French Railroads for the Allied war effort. He was given the rank of brigadier general to command cooperation with his efforts, and ever afterward, he was known as 'General Atterbury.' Among other accomplishments, General Atterbury is credited with establishing the regional management system which was adopted by the Pennsy in 1920.

The stock market was booming in 1928. The Van Swerigen brothers, entrepreneurial investors in Northern central and Northeastern rail lines, had started a public securities company called Allegheny Corporation for the purpose of buying into and playing the very active market of the time with stocks of specific railroads. The investment-minded public, swept up in the twenties mentality of quick sensational profits, immediately bought $83 million in subscriptions to this enterprise. This atmosphere of 'buy, buy, buy!' was soon to end disastrously in the long, gloomy period known as the Great Depression.

The Pennsy too, riding a several year upswing, organized its own securities company for the purpose of

Previous pages: The yard and trainshed at Broad Street station in Philadelphia, circa 1935. *Above:* These ads appeared in 1945, when the war was almost won. *At right:* The post-war sun shone, and Pennsy liners like the *Broadway Limited* had vacationers on the move.

making railroad investments on the behalf of its stockholders. This entity, known as 'The Pennroad Corporation,' specifically emphasized solid investments, and was held under the trusteeship of General Atterbury and two other Pennsy executives.

Pennsy stockholders acquired over 80 percent of Pennroad's stock at $15 per share at a 'one for two' stock ratio. Realized capital from this sale was $91.1 million. The salient feature of this plan was that Pennroad created no funded debt; the Pennsy itself did not *invest* in Pennroad—stockholders both funded and reaped the benefits of the program, and the railroad got to reap the benefits of being the parent of the acquiring company of some very useful properties.

Pennroad invested heavily in the Detroit, Toledo & Ironton Railroad, a heavy feeder of Detroit traffic to several trunk lines; and in the Canton Company of Baltimore, which owned valuable waterfront property in Baltimore. Both of these organizations had existing, mutually advantageous relationships with the Pennsy.

The Seaboard Airline Railway, the New Haven, the Boston & Maine and the Pittsburgh & West Virginia were also acquired either in whole or in part.

The Crash of 1929 followed very shortly after Pennroad's $38 million purchase of the Pittsburgh & West Virginia, and this would have dealt a crippling blow to the investment company's finances had not Pennroad

All Aboard...

FOR A HAPPY VACATION

GO BY TRAIN!

CHOOSE your own vacationland .:. but for extra pleasure . . . go by train!

It's much more enjoyable. And the train is so comfortable, convenient and dependable. There's room to roam, room to relax . . . whether you go coach or Pullman. Your carefree vacation starts the moment you step aboard any one of the 1100 daily trains that make up Pennsylvania Railroad's great passenger fleets. No matter where you're bound, there's a train ready to take you on the day you plan to go.

Courteous Pennsylvania Railroad employes are on hand to serve you when you make the initial arrangements of your travel details, when you are boarding the train and en route. This year—for the vacation of your dreams—take a happy, carefree trip . . . *Take the Pennsylvania!*

PENNSYLVANIA RAILROAD

Visit the CHICAGO RAILROAD FAIR June 25 to October 2, 1949

had the foresight to issue an additional, underwritten stock offering, which as of the Crash was 50 percent taken up; the underwriters had to finance the remaining 50 percent, or $22.3 million of the entire offering.

Pennroad would be an investment company for Pennsy stockholders for some time to come. To ensure continuity and stability of management, seven Pennsy directors were selected to serve on the board of Pennroad.

In this same period, the Pennsy vastly increased its operating efficiency by increasing the average freight tonnage per train. This was made possible by the increasing use of steel in car design, which allowed for bigger cars with higher weight to volume ratios. Freight tonnage rose steadily from 839 tons per average freight train in 1921 to a peak tonnage of 1905 in 1929, tapering off slightly in the early 1930s to rise again in 1934 to 1006 tons per train.

At the same time, Pennsy trains were moving steadily faster and gross ton-miles per train (which represents the rate of freight movement measured in tonnage per miles traveled) rose 42 percent.

From 1925 to 1929, passenger revenues fell by some $15 million. Other modes of transportation were making themselves felt—in particular, America's love affair with the automobile was being given heavy promotion by Henry Ford's cheap, reliable Model T. Airplanes were, toward the end of the decade, to start making their long-haul presence known as well. Atterbury was not averse to investing in the burgeoning airline industry. By 1927, mass air transportation was deemed practicable, both by investors and the general public.

The Pennsy joined forces with the Wright Aeronautical Company, the Curtis Aeroplane and Motor Company, National Aviation Corporation and a banking investment group in New York. Together, they incorporated Transcontinental Air Transport, Inc.

The system linked together thusly: a westbound passenger rode the Pennsy from New York City to Columbus, Ohio, there boarding a plane bound for a western connection with the Santa Fe Railroad, and upon the Santa Fe's arrival at Clovis, New Mexico, another plane would fly said passenger to Los Angeles or San Francisco.

The first Transcontinental Air Transport (TAT) trip across country was made on 7 July 1929. Despite the economic malaise of 1930, the company's Ford Trimotors were flying two schedules each way early in that year. By the end of 1932, the company had inaugurated an all-air 24 hour service coast to coast—and though the Pennsy continued to offer its ground service as an alternative along its section of the company's route, the writing was obviously on the wall.

TAT was reorganized to consolidate its mail and passenger operations, which resulted in a new company—Transcontinental and Western Air, Inc. President Franklin Delano Roosevelt canceled all airmail contracts in 1934, but the Pennsy held onto its one-fifth interest in the venture until 1936, at which time the investment had lost all interest for the Pennsy, as the road could not further its railroad business by the connection. Transcontinental and Western Air was to eventually evolve into Trans World Airways.

The Pennsy on the Highways

The Pennsy also invested in numerous trucking companies to handle short haul, less-than carload burdenage. Motor trucks were forming an increasingly tough competition for small loads, and the Pennsy looked back to the methods of the old Camden & Amboy to 'beat the heat.' The use of containers for freight and luggage had been operating procedure on the old C&A, as is discussed elsewhere in this text. This helped with

At first, the Pennsy considered diesel power to be just one of several options. *Below* is a 1940s Pennsy attempt to harness steam power in a new way—the steam turbine; turbine blades, not pistons, turned the wheels. The S2, shown here, weighed over one million pounds with its tender, and generated 65,000 lbs of tractive force.

the short-load problem, as five or six containers could be loaded onto a flatcar, and the car could thus be burdened with a diversity of freight which otherwise would have taken up several cars.

Trucks also served in Pennsy 'station to station' duty, inaugurated in 1923. With the use of motor trucks, many stops could be made along a route, and the packages and boxes thus gathered could be brought to central points for sorting and delivery.

The major truck lines involved in Pennsy operation were Pennsylvania Truck Lines, Inc (formerly Pennsylvania Transfer Company of Pittsburgh), Scott Brothers (and its subsidiary, Peninsula Auto Express) of Philadelphia and Trenton, and Baltimore Transfer Company.

In addition to the savings recognized by the use of trucks for short hauls, the Pennsy's new, more powerful locomotives and larger tenders could make longer runs without maintenance, and fueling stops than the older running gear; due to these advantages, 19 operating yards were closed down. A large number of train stops were eliminated by the advent of a new freight classification system whereby, rather than the old reshuffling of train cars according to their individual pinpoint destinations at each division line, special through trains were scheduled from origin to destination for a select few destination points.

The Pennsy dabbled in buses, too. Seeing the decline in passenger traffic in the 1920s, much of which was due to motorcars and such, the railroad considered doing away with some of its less profitable passenger lines and replacing them with bus lines! The Pennsy bought into several motor bus companies, among which was the Motor Transit Corporation, which ran buses between New York and Chicago, and was expanding into the West and the South. It was 1928, and the bus line soon changed its name to the Greyhound Corporation.

In January of 1931, the Greyhound Corporation and the Pennsy consolidated operations of parallel lines into the Pennsylvania Greyhound Lines. The Pennsy acquired the entire preferred stock issue and 50 percent of the common of this new company. Terminal facilities were shared in many places, operations were coordinated and the savings of substituting bus for rail passenger service (in certain locations) was estimated, as of 1930, to be half a million dollars per year.

The Pennsy developed its own bus lines for a while, too. These were the Pennsylvania General Transit Company and the Pennsylvania; Illinois; Indiana; and Virginia General Transit companies. In addition to this, a number of small bus lines were purchased outright.

Other Improvements

Pennsy 'regional system' mileage declined from 11,108 to 10,573 as a result of trimming unprofitable operations from the company.

The Philadelphia Pennsy station and lines had been de-congested by the electrification of the road's lines to Paoli and Chestnut Hill, which resulted in faster running. The Broad Street station train shed had burnt down in 1923, so a new station was planned across the Schuylkill, in West Philadelphia. This station was begun in 1925 and completed in 1926. It was a 14-story building located at 32nd and Market Streets.

A 'suburban' station in the heart of Philadelphia was put into service on 8 September 1930. Its seven station tracks and four large passenger platforms were built below street level; electrification of the commuter lines made that possible. The office building that was built on top of this complex lay between 16th and 17th Streets and was 22 stories tall. The Pennsy's executive offices moved into this station in mid-1930.

This classically designed passenger terminal faced the

Schuylkill. Four of its tracks and two of its passenger platforms were built for New York-Washington passenger traffic, while on an upper level suburban tracks ran at right angles to these. Corinthian columns 11 feet in diameter and 71 feet high filled the huge porticos on the station building's east and west faces.

Unfortunately, the old elevated track platforms to Broad Street remained, as the city, contracted to tear them down, was incapacitated by the Depression; the notorious 'Chinese Wall' remained.

The entire line from New York to Washington was electrified, with government help, as it was felt that the project would—and it did—create jobs. Through electric passenger service on the New York-Washington route was inaugurated on 10 February 1935, and through electric freight service began in June of 1935. The travel time of the Pennsy's *Congressional Limited* passenger lines was cut from 4 1/4 to 3 3/4 hours, and many New York-Philadelphia trains made their runs in one hour and 40 minutes—a considerable saving in time over steam engines.

'General' William Atterbury retired on 24 April 1935. Stepping into his shoes was yet another Pennsy president who had worked his way up through the ranks, beginning his Pennsy career in the engineering corps. This man, who became vice president under Atterbury following the death of Elisha Lee, was Martin W Clement.

Electrification

Line electrification had proven to be so much more efficient for some areas than steam power that the process was extended to the lines from Harrisburg to New York, Philadelphia and Perryville, which work was accomplished with ease—as were the earlier electrification projects. The increased manpower available via government programs, and the eagerness of the government to promote job-creating projects, was certainly a factor.

These electrification projects were completed in April of 1938. Of course, with the use of electric traction locomotives, facilities had to be altered and methods of train handling changed. But the main feat of electrification was the speeding up of both passenger and freight service.

The *Broadway Limited*'s time from New York to Chicago was reduced from 18 hours before 1932 to 16 hours flat as of 15 June 1938. Fares fell, too, as they were based on hourly rates for trips of less than 28 hours. Electrification went well with the use of new, lightweight passenger cars designed by the Pullman Company.

The *Spirit of St Louis*, another Pennsy flyer, had cut two and a half hours from its westbound run, and the *Congressional Limited* cut its already speedy run by 40 minutes. Freight service was likewise speeded up—for instance, Florida-New York delivery time was cut from four to three days. The average time between New York and the Enola yard at Harrisburg was cut by two hours.

Small-load freight operations were improved by an increase, in the Pennsy's motor trucking operations, of over 6000 miles from 1935 to 1945, and an additional 1224 motor freight stations built in the same period.

The Pennsy also pioneered free pickup and delivery to points beyond 260 miles.

Legislation and Regulation

The Great Depression spurred a nationwide surge of public works projects, sponsored by President Roosevelt's WPA, a child of his 'New Deal' social programs. Other spawn of the Roosevelt era was legislation dealing directly with the 'railroad problem.'

One of these programs provided for the public regulation of railroad holding companies, the continuation of government loans for railroad improvements (in the form of Reconstruction Finance Corporation loans), the revamping of federal laws governing railroad receiverships, ICC regulation of competing motor carriers, cooperation between railroads for the reduction of wasteful duplication and competition, and the consummation of proposed railroad consolidations if such were in the public interest and followed the guidelines of the law. In addition to this, Congress extended the Bankruptcy Act to include railroads, thereby expediting reorganizations.

The second of these programs, in brief, was the Emergency Railroad Transportation Act of 1933. This law allowed joint use of terminals and tracks, controlled service allowances to shippers and generally provided means to avoid waste and unnecessary operations expense.

Motor carriers heretofore were unregulated, and hence charged lower rates than the railroads, which inevitably left the rail carriers with only the lowest forms of carriage. The Eastman Act was passed in 1935, which specifically set up freight rates for motor carriers much the same as those set up for the railroads.

The nation's second lapse into deep depression in 1938 spawned yet more rail regulation. After carefully weighing the information brought before him by various reporting committees and organizations, President Roosevelt set up a 'Committee of Six,' composed of three representatives of railroad management and three of railroad labor, to study the precarious position many railroads found themselves in.

Several acts were submitted to Congress as a result of the committee's report, yet the most important result of the committee's recommendations was the Transportation Act of 1940.

This act replied to grievances aired by the Association of American Railroads in a 'Railroad Program' they'd submitted to President Roosevelt in 1938. This 'Program' requested relief from various federally-imposed taxes, equal treatment of all forms of transportation, relief from federal and state 'make work' measures (which limited the number of cars per train and required 'by the book' crew complements for even the shortest run by the smallest train), that the ICC consider fair business profits returns to the railroads when setting rate limits.

The Transportation Act of 1940 was composed of three sections or 'titles', the first amending the existing

The ad at right touts the Pennsy's very great contribution to the US World War II effort. Note the list of materials hauled, and the apology for passenger delays. This crushing traffic, combined with deferred repairs, engendered very serious equipment problems.

KEEPING APPOINTMENTS WITH CONVOYS

In a day's combat, an infantry division fires about 300 tons of ammunition ... 100 37 mm. anti-aircraft guns, 127½ tons ... and the thousands of army vehicles "passing the ammunition" and other supplies each burn up an average of 10 gallons of gasoline ...

All of these materials — the guns, the "gas", the ammunition, the vehicles — *plus 700,000 other different military items*—must come by sea.

A gigantic supply task without parallel in the history of the nation, this job calls for the finest coordination of American railroads with ships.

The railroads must bring everything to ship sidings exactly as needed — and when needed. Any slip, any delay, may hold up a convoy sailing.

So keeping appointments with convoys is one of the most important jobs railroads have these days.

If pushing a "convoy train" through ahead of your passenger train caused you to be a little late for an early-morning business appointment, the Pennsylvania Railroad feels sure you will gladly overlook it. The demands of war must have not only railroad equipment—but the right-of-way!

★ 37,028 *in the Armed Forces*
★ 71 *have given their lives for their country*

BUY UNITED STATES WAR BONDS AND STAMPS

PENNSYLVANIA RAILROAD
Serving the Nation

Above: Sunnyside yard in the late 1930s—note the GG-1 loco here. The Pennsy's electrification program got a very trying workout during World War II, even with the many improvements of the 1930s. *At left:* Pennsy's 30th Street Philadelphia station, complete with sailors coming and going, in the passenger- and freight-heavy early 1940s.

law, the second regulating water carriers and the third, composed of miscellaneous provisions.

This Act positively solved the problems enumerated in the Railroad Program, with the exceptions of letting the ICC continue to make inconsiderately low rates, and certain rates were as yet free from ICC regulation.

In addition to this, government regulation came to bear in wage increases, passenger fare reductions, pension plans and union disputes.

In general, federal regulation in the late 1930s both helped and hindered railroads. In 1938, many roads felt the terrible crunch of the 1930s 'second depression.' Yet, they were grateful for the legislative gains they had been granted.

Gearing Up For War

The Pennsy's electrification of many lines enabled the release to other areas of operation the steam locos that had been displaced by the electrics.

In addition, 7000 freight cars were built with borrowed WPA funds in 1934. In 1935, 10,000 more cars were built. By 1938, 3838 more cars would be added to Pennsy freight stock.

When war raged in Europe in 1939, the Pennsy,

thinking ahead, ordered 2500 new freight cars, and 80,000 tons of rail. The new cars ordered were of stronger construction than the thousands of cars they replaced. In keeping with the Pennsy's program of 'operating efficiency,' they were not only structurally stronger, but had greater capacity. Fewer cars could carry more; yet the tocsin of war called the Pennsy to renovate 17,500 already retired gondolas and boxcars.

In 1940, 4500 more freight cars were ordered, and five new electric passenger locos were also ordered. No extraordinary physical plant improvements were made, save for some rail replacement and track changes at the Enola yard, a new engine terminal at Harrisburg, a larger coal dumping facility at the Sandusky port on Lake Erie and the installation at various points on the road of advanced signaling equipment to handle the soon-to-be-heavier rail traffic.

World War II

No matter what preparations for heavier traffic were made, no rail line could have foreseen the intense usage that America's railroads—especially the eastern roads—were to receive. Making what would be in peacetime not only a lucrative but very maintenance-expensive situation very dicey was the fact that most roads, including the Pennsy, essentially abandoned equipment maintenance 'for the duration.'

Two major factors in this intensive traffic were also reasons for the railroads' outstanding wartime success in handling such. Roosevelt asked the heads of various railroad companies to inform his government as to how railroads should best be utilized and operated in times of war. Pennsy President Clement helped with this report, whose recommendations gave birth to the Office of Defense Transportation, which had authority to divert traffic and to take other actions to clear freight and passenger 'logjams' at any point and at any time. The roads were quite prepared to cooperate with one another now, having seen the disasters of the past, and were permitted to govern themselves by their own Association of American Railroads; thus the AAR was a roaring success in terms of coordinating shipment schedules and using facilities. Other preparations included the building, in the mid-thirties, of government-owned freight warehouses, so that freight cars in wartime would not again be wasted as wheeled storage sheds, caught in freight gridlocks at major ports. The idea was to keep things moving at all points, so that Allied forces were constantly barraged with supplies, reinforcements and other needed battle supplies.

The Pennsy's motive power supply was ample for the task, consisting of steam locos in great abundance, including new, experimental four-cylinder freight locos of tremendous power, and a great abundance—some 261 passenger, freight and switcher types—of electric locomotives. The government released materials for building freight locos, but not for passenger locos during the war—a factor that 'would only further damage rail passenger capabilities later.

Thousands of old freight cars were revamped at tremendous expense, owing to the civilian dearth of building materials (most of which were channeled to direct military usage). Again, passenger traffic, which

had increased fourfold during the war years, was of secondary concern to federal authorities in charge of allocations, and the Pennsy was not allowed to build a single passenger coach. This meant that the full-to-bursting passenger cars already in service were taking a tremendous beating from the steady influx of soldiers, their loved ones going to visit them and the general crushing load created by the very active presence of the major military facilities which were present all over the east coast at that time.

The Pennsy's wartime freight traffic was 40 percent higher than it had been even in booming 1929, and in some sections of the Pennsy system the increase was 60 to 100 percent greater.

Passenger travel on the New York-Washington line hit a peak on 24 December 1943 of 260 percent that of the heaviest peak day ever before.

Shipping facilities were enlarged and upgraded to handle freight and personnel going to Europe. South Amboy, Jersey City, Greenville, Waverly, Newark and Philadelphia were some of the freight yards and dock facilities which were improved to handle the war's tremendous volumes.

New tracks and yards were built, and complete rehabilitations of secondary lines were effected in order to serve boot camps, training centers and the many war industries that needed heavy transport availability.

These were improvements made for the contingencies of war. They would prove cumbersome afterward. The Pennsy sank almost $40 million into wartime road improvements; equipment improvements soaked up $195 million.

The use of equipment during this time was costly—maintenance was deferred; cars were kept running with repairs of expedience, track was repaired only as absolutely needed; the vast improvements noted above were of the same ilk—normally, attention spent on the new facilities would have been matched by upkeep system-wide. The system had that 'broken down' look at the end of the war, and so did its finance.

Adding to this burden was the federal Excess Profits Tax Law, which was designed to prevent war profiteering. This law levied a 90 percent tax on all profits which were deemed to be 'above normal.' The prospective taxpayer could figure his debt by either averaging net income for the years 1936–39 (minus five percent) or could compute tax owed on the basis of invested capital.

Since most railroads had absolutely terrible financial years in the 1930s, they chose the invested capital method. The Pennsy, whose 1936–39 record was worse than its post-World War I record, followed suit. This method allowed earnings of eight percent on invested capital up to $5 million, and seven percent on amounts above that. The 'bite' on this method came from stipulation that borrowed—or 'funded debt'—capital be included at only half its true amount, which, for the Pennsy, whose funded debt made up two-thirds of its capitalization, was a serious reduction of permissible earnings.

Several other stipulations further reduced permissible earnings—it seemed that the federal tax men wanted to *hurt* the railroads, but that was never a stated case. The Pennsy's 1944 tax bill was a company record 15.13 cents per revenue dollar.

THE END

Post War

The Pennsy's business continued to boom traffic-wise in 1946. But while it was a boom time for carriage, it was the worst year in Pennsy history; for the first time in 100 years of operation, the company operated at a deficit.

Wage increases granted at mid-year were made retroactive to the first of the year by federal edict. Rate increases— badly needed to cover deferred maintenance— were delayed until year end. The road operated under the as-yet unrelieved wartime limitations of labor and the high cost of materials, with the added complications brought about by the peacetime boom.

Dividends were paid at three percent, and that was only possible by way of past years' earnings. Employees made more money, but the Pennsy was losing money at a record rate. Operating revenues were $867 million, and operating expenses were $876 million.

Pennsy improvements in this year saw the inauguration of through passenger service from New York, Philadelphia, Baltimore, and Washington to San Francisco, Los Angeles, El Paso and San Antonio. This was made possible through line usage agreements with various western and southwestern railroads. Various improvements were also made throughout the Pennsy system, involving trackage, terminals, cars and locomotives.

High-speed four-cylinder passenger locomotives, designed in the late 1930s, but whose production was delayed by the war, were finally delivered in full quantity— the last 36 of an original 1945 order of 50— in 1946. These were soon joined by another harbinger of changing times: eight 7500 horsepower locomotives in the diesel electric mode, tests run on two diesels in 1945 having proven successful.

In addition, hundreds of new boxcars and gondola cars were built at the Altoona shops, and hundreds of new passenger coaches, including sleeping, dining, lounge and observation cars joined the Pennsy's passenger fleet.

Due to increased freight rates, the Pennsy recognized record freight revenues, but because of rising material costs and huge maintenance costs borne of wartime deferred maintenance, the Pennsy would still not rise effectually far from 'the red.'

In 1947, the Pennsy squeaked by with operating revenues of $957 million versus expenses of $950 million.

The year 1948 saw the Pennsy's largest peacetime revenues in its history, due mainly to service rate increases granted across the board by the federal government. However, freight rates were still almost down to the 1921 level, and employee wages were more than double what they had been in that period.

Operating revenues were $1.04 billion and expenses were $1.01 billion. The Pennsy management was still shaken by the trough of 1946.

The Long Island Railroad was a special thorn: the Pennsy had been losing millions on the short-haul, less-than carload freight and passenger trade, and the Long Island was its most costly affiliate, losing $6.02 million in 1948 alone. The Pennsy commended the Long Island to the American Contract and Trust Company, a Pennsy subsidiary, which bought the Long Island's obligations. In effect, the Pennsy commended the Long Island to the courts.

A pact with the city transit system of Philadelphia enabled the Pennsy to build new tracks, abandoning the old Broad Street station and the civically infamous 'Chinese Wall.' Improvements on the line between Pittsburgh and Columbus were made to effect a savings in freight operations in those areas.

The hit of the year in 1948 was the delivery of 359 out of an order of 590 diesel-electric locomotives. Dieselization was well under way on all principal freight and passenger lines. Diesels had proven more generally reliable, maintenance-wise, than steam locos.

Many of the Pennsy's headliner trains, the *General*, the *Liberty Limited*, the *Spirit of St Louis*, the *Pittsburgher*, the *Golden Triangle*, the *Cincinnati Limited* and the *Penn Texas*, were renovated with diesel power and new diner, kitchen-dormitory, and cabin sleeper cars.

The Buying Group of Railroads, a railroad cooperative company, bought the stock of the Pullman Company. Each railroad in the Buying Group— and the Pennsy was a member of this organization— had the right to take possession, from the Pullman stock, of the standard model of sleeping cars used on its line.

Cars were normally leased from Pullman, and this 1948 purchase effectively gave the Pennsy the 465 cars assigned to its line service. These cars were virtually the same appearance-wise as the newer, lighter weight cars, so the Pennsy, considering that diesel power compensated for any weight disadvantage, decided to do mild renovation on these acquired cars, at a savings.

Freight car shortages brought about by World War II overuse were finally equalized, and less-than carload freight was handled economically by the building of special boxcars which could carry, without damage, wide assortments of kinds of freight, thereby filling a few cars with what would have incompletely used many cars in the past.

Still, this was not enough. The year 1949 saw operating revenues of $903 million versus expense totaling $891 million. Labor strikes in the coal and steel industries cut deep into Pennsy loadage in those areas, and wage increases, higher fuel and materials costs and the ever-present specter of repairs delayed during the war cost the railroad millions.

The Pennsy's post-war equipment improvements program was to cost $325 million total, of which $212 million went to freight equipment. The Pennsy's holdings of 820 diesel locomotives in freight, passenger and switcher configurations totaled 1,433,490 horsepower— the most diesel hp of any railroad in the world at the time.

The Pennsy obviously was being optimistic, but was pursuing the course of trying to *build* itself out of debt— as per the above concerning dieselization in the face of increasing instability on the part of its main breadwinners, the steel and coal industries. Pittsburgh, despite all changes the years had wrought, remained the road's emblem of success: that city symbolized the industrial Northeast, which had fed, and grown with, the phenomenal growth of the Pennsy.

Previous pages: Titans: An M1 (left) and an I1 at the Enola yards. *Above:* The Pennsy's *Broadway Limited* races its old competitor, the NYC's *20th Century Limited*, across the Illinois flatlands in 1946.

The advent of the 40 hour work week caused weekend shut-downs of Pennsy freight operations. Over two-thirds of Pennsy revenues came from freight operations.

Increased passenger fares helped defray the costs of new passenger equipment, which shared the fate of the Pennsy's freight equipment; business was down. The nine years from 1940–1949 saw wages increase by 104 percent, and increasing numbers of railroad employee groups were requesting 48 hours' pay for 40 hour weeks.

On 16 June 1949, MW Clement was elected Chairman of the Pennsy board of directors, and Walter S Franklin stepped into the Pennsy presidency.

Labor difficulties continued into 1951, and concomitant work stoppages further rocked Pennsy revenues.

On 27 August 1950, the federal government seized control of American railroads in the face of a threatened nationwide strike by rail workers.

Even so, the Pennsy joined forces with the Wabash in acquiring the Detroit, Toledo & Ironton Railroad from the Pennsy holding company, Pennroad. This move, it was hoped, would consolidate freight traffic in the vital Midwest for both the Pennsy and the Wabash.

The Pennsy expanded its passenger and freight dieselization program to a total expenditure of $534 mil-lion. Corporate income tax rates went up in 1950, and a new excess profits tax was also enacted.

Government control was relinquished on 23 May 1952. With the exception of a bright spot created by the development of TrucTrain service, which was a form of container hauling in which the containers were actually truck trailers, the moderate successes and steady downward spiral of the road's fortunes continued until 1957. JM Symes was now the Pennsy president—having stepped into Franklin's shoes in 1954. Inflation and not-so-terrific freight rates were rasping away at railroad morale.

The year 1957 broke the camel's back. The Pennsy had been a giant suffering a serious injury, but had chances of getting better. A serious business recession in 1957 alarmed railroads nationwide, but the event, in the words of President Symes, '...struck the Pennsylvania Railroad with severe and unexpected force.'

Railroads had been begging Congress for better rate structures, and now the government was taking a closer look at it. For the Pennsy, though, the situation was absolutely terrible—a big deficit was further compounded by disastrous snow storms in 1958 which cost the Pennsy freight business $10 million. The deficit in early 1958 was $25 million. President Symes—perhaps the first overt Pennsy pessimist in the head office—termed 1958 as 'one of the most difficult in the history of the company—even more difficult than the depression years of the 1930s.'

The new age. *Left:* This 1953 Electro Motive E8 2250 hp diesel wore the keystone logo, the Pennsy's famous Tuscan red paint, and had the same natty pinstriping that many a GG-1 still wore. *Above:* The Pennsy replaced their P5A electrics with 5000 hp E-44s like this in 1960.

Merger discussions

In 1957, the Pennsy and the New York Central undertook a study in consideration of consolidating their operations—a merger of the once proud competitors.

Symes became chairman of the board in 1960, and Allen Greenough became president. While Pennsy rolling stock was upgraded—new electric freight locomotives were bought, the Pennsy's always understated but ever-present New York Harbor operations were modernized by the purchase of seven new diesel tugboats, and TrucTrain operations were expanding via a pooled stock of 6000 specially-designed cars—1960 operating revenues were $144 million under the figures for 1957! Sinking like a stone, the road paid a 25 cent dividend—and Pennsy stockholders, poor souls, endorsed wholeheartedly a proposed merger with the similarly-ailing New York Central.

The next few years saw the Pennsy and the NYC awaiting ICC approval of their plan, but the writing was on the wall: two giants, inextricably bound up with northeastern industry, and unable to see the necessity of paring down enough to survive the turbulent times that were now upon them.

Eastern railroads were more convoluted than railroads elsewhere in the US: they had complex, very expensive physical plants—the very nature of the east's rolling countryside insured that a road of any size would resemble a skein of tangled thread on a map. They were bulky systems, designed to be fed by ore, coal and heavy industry and they were caught in their own enormousness.

Pennsy Station Goes Down

In 1962, the Pennsy announced plans to raze Pennsy Station in Manhattan, to build a relatively cheap station underneath the Madison Square Garden, which would be built where Pennsy Station then stood—the Pennsy wanted to sell the property, and in 1964, Pennsy Station was gone. Symbolic of what the Pennsy's power had come to mean—access, for everyone, to the wide, wide reaches of the USA—Pennsy station was gone!

And fittingly so, sadly so. The Pennsy itself was disappearing. But things looked 'hopeful' for a few years yet—the end, though, did come. The two roads did merge. The Pennsy should have the last word here.

The Chairman's Last Letter

The following is Stuart T Saunders, the Pennsy's last chairman of the board, addressing Pennsy stockholders in the yearly report for 1966. Though Pennsy was 'in the black,' its time had come.

'The Chairman's Letter

...Our 28.8 percent rise in consolidated earnings and 33 percent gain in railroad earnings were gratifying. The most significant progress toward the long-range strengthening of our Company, however, was unanimous approval by the Interstate Commerce Commission of our merger with the New York Central Railroad.

The proposed Penn Central merger in 1966 reached the point where its eventual consummation seems certain. Delay has resulted from requests for an injunction staying the effective date....The United States Supreme Court has heard an appeal from the lower court decision on an unusually expeditious schedule, and now has the case under consideration.

In argument before the Supreme Court, the Department of Justice announced for the first time that the United States Government believes the merger is in the public interest and should be consummated promptly....The primary issue before the Court is whether the ICC acted properly in granting permission for the Penn Central merger to become effective before (1) the commission has formulated conditions protecting the Erie-Lackawanna and Delaware & Hudson railroads against possible losses as a result of our merger or (2) these railroads are included in a major Eastern system....

The Pennsylvania and the New York Central, by virtue of careful joint planning, are prepared to start combined operations immediately.

The Penn Central merger will...provide the first-class railroad service and the financial strength necessary for keeping pace with the transportation needs of American industry.

...We have already pumped much new lifeblood into our operations through the outlay of more than half a billion dollars in the past few years for new equipment and modernized facilities....We registered gains during 1966 in important categories of freight traffic. These included piggyback, new automobiles and iron ore, as well as grain, coal, semi-finished steel and other trainload and multiple-car shipments. Our Marketing Department is helping to develop new sources of traffic and is devising ways of building volume from our customers.

We are vigorously promoting a new concept of railroad passenger service, based on developing modern medium-range and short-range operations as a supplement to other modes of transportation....It will enable railroads to make significant contributions toward solving the pressing problems of traffic congestion, air pollution, safety and mounting costs of highway construction within and between metropolitan areas.

In cooperation with the US Department of Transportation, the Pennsylvania is building a modern, high-speed passenger line between New York and Washington. This will begin operation in the latter part of 1967...we are continuing to work closely with the Southeastern Pennsylvania Transportation Authority, the Commonwealth of Pennsylvania, the State of New Jersey and other local and regional governmental entities in financing new equipment and improving frequency and quality of commuter service.

This type of contribution toward an integrated national transportation system,...offers the best hope for reducing our persistent passenger deficits.

The Pennsylvania welcomes the establishment of the Federal Department of Transportation....We are confident that the Department of Transportation will make a fresh appraisal of the capabilities of the railroads for both passenger and freight service. We pledge our full cooperation to this Department...in constructive efforts to create a balanced national transportation.

Our recently acquired non-railroad subsidiary companies, described in this report, contributed more than $16 million to 1966 consolidated earnings, demonstrating the soundness of our program of diversifying our sources of income.

Concurrently, we are pushing development of the

Shown *at top* is one of the last locomotives built by Baldwin for the Pennsy—a 2400 hp RT-624 center cab diesel freight engine. Baldwin ceased locomotive building operations in the mid-1950s. *Above left:* This 2000 hp Fairbanks-Morse locomotive was another type of power in use on the Pennsy in the early 1950s. *Above:* Pennsy GE DP4 electrics.

profit potential of air rights and urban property adjacent to our railroad facilities. We are launching several new industrial parks as sources of additional freight traffic....1967...promises to be a difficult year...we are confronted with an increase of at least $30 million in wage and employee benefit costs....If the national economy remains strong, we believe that 1967 will be another good year for the Pennsylvania and the railroad industry generally.'

In 1968, The New York Central and the Pennsylvania merged operations.

THE PENN CENTRAL AND CONRAIL

Merger

The merger of the two old competitors was anything but smooth. The Pennsy had been suffering badly since the 1940s, and bad as its economic woes were, its organizational structure was also badly tangled—this was the legacy of the long-standing Pennsy philosophy of being the 'railroader's railroad.' Management was fine insofar as it had to do directly with running the railroad, and Pennsy's top executives had often enough been railroad men, 'raised up from the ground' in good, solid, technical railroading expertise. But now that both federal and state governments were heavily favoring private transportation—highways, both state and interstate, were being built at unprecedented rates in the 1960s—and there seemed no chance of getting the government to allow the Pennsy to trim away trackage that had long been useless, the gargantuan railroad seemed about to drown in its own gravy; it needed new ideas, fresh ideas—maybe even a change in its fundamental operational mind.

The New York Central had already begun a 'renaissance' under the leadership of Alfred Perlman, whose singlemindedness ran in another direction; it was his desire to renovate the NYC's entire system, and he and his assistants pored over the line's accounting records, unearthing mistakes and errors that had cost the ailing NYC millions. The NYC actually was optimistic, even in its darkest hours—Perlman's bright young men were making the road more efficient, while the Pennsy, their age-old competitor, was still doing things the old way, which relied upon massive amounts of ready funding. The Pennsy no longer had that funding, and the very passenger operations that had been the Pennsy's pride in the past were dragging it down. The ICC was not responsive to requests for permission to cut dead wood from Pennsy lines.

Pennsy chairman Symes and NYC chairman Robert Young met in 1957 'to talk deficits,' and made it very clear that the context for these talks was merger. Perlman hated it—he and his experts viewed the world of Pennsy-NYC merger as one in which the larger and more assets-heavy Pennsy would be the senior partner in any such deal, and the NYC and its interests would be held under the thumb of Philadelphia parochialism—and, by cracky, their fears were ultimately justified!

Symes, on the other hand, hated the thought nearly as badly—perhaps even more. Symes was a pure-bred Pennsy man, all the way from starting out as a ticket agent to living on the Main Line and being an Anglo-Saxon Protestant. His railroad had been, not even arguably, but just plain been, the most important railroad in the world, and continued to be, even in its death throes. Here he was, he who had hoped to pass on the baton to yet another man who had worked his way up solidly, on the verge of throwing in with his railroad's most hated enemy! It was an admission on the part of both roads—they were simply too far gone to go on alone. However, Symes and Young got along rather well, as men tend to do when they are dangled together over an abyss.

A merger was not in the works for 1958. Alfred Perlman stalled, saying that such a huge merger 'might

Previous pages: A yard full of Conrail diesel power at Conway, PA. *Above:* In this late 1970s photo, former Penn Central locomotives are being painted with a temporary 'CR' to signify 'Conrail.' Amidst several 3000 hp Alco C-430 road switchers are two 3000 hp EMD GP-40s (third and fourth from right, with and without radiator 'wing' cowling).

not be in the public interest.' He intimated that government opposition might ensue. A study was conducted which showed that a savings of $100 million could result from such a merger, but by that time, Robert Young had died, and Perlman, riding a temporary high in the NYC's earnings, called off negotiations until a later date—the NYC was on an upswing and Perlman wanted to ensure that the NYC would be the senior partner in any merger. He turned from the Pennsy and went to talk merger with the B&O and the C&O, saying that the three of them could form a 'counterweight' to the Pennsy. These two roads were not interested, and when the B&O agreed to merge with the C&O, Perlman tried to disrupt the merger by buying stock on the B&O—a proxy war ensued in which Perlman was defeated.

While this was taking place, Stuart Saunders of the N&W, a Pennsy-controlled company, sought to acquire the Nickel Plate and lease the Wabash—this would

create a rail colossus directly aimed at NYC territory, and Perlman angrily petitioned the ICC for permission to take part in this merger. Saunders in turn was angered, as was Symes. Inclusion of the Central in the N&W/Nickel Plate/Wabash combination was vigorously opposed. The merger went through and the NYC was left out in the cold. Time was running out, and Perlman was grasping at straws— he was realized that the NYC could not write its own ticket.

Symes accused Perlman of evading the real issue, which was the merger with the Pennsy. Merger fever was gaining steam; the N&W complex was drawing near the newly merged C&O, and several weaker roads sought merger with the extremely healthy N&W.

Symes knew that the NYC would have to accept any offer the Pennsy made— accept or sink. So, two men who did not trust each other met— and hashed out a merger proposal. The voting setup of the new company would be 60 percent Pennsy to 40 percent NYC; the NYC would sell its B&O stock and the Pennsy, likewise, its N&W stock. The Central would merge into the Pennsy, and Perlman's nightmare had come true. In 1963, Symes was ready to retire, and none other than Stuart Saunders stepped in to fill his shoes.

Saunders and Perlman could not agree on strategy, tactics or even what this new company would actually be. Besides this, they sincerely disliked one another.

Perlman and Saunders

The vagaries of the nation's financial climate weighed heavy on freight-rich roads like the NYC and the Pennsy; their passenger operations were deemed essential by the federal government— especially in the case of the Pennsy; but being the nation's number one people mover that did not bring sufficient monetary returns. The railroads had ceased being the most important transportation entities in the US; they all knew it, and it was beginning to dawn (not nearly fast enough) on the US government.

Yet, for a railroad in serious financial straights, which would need millions in reserve capital to succeed in the proposed merger, the Pennsy seemed intent on expensive, very long term investments. Saunders had been impressed by the various conglomerates such as IT&T, Litton Industries and Gulf and Western that seemed to be flourishing in the 1960s. Why not use the Pennsy as the most important of the company's holdings and

At left: Commuter service such as the *Metroliner* was extremely successful, but Penn Central's revenues disappeared down the tracks even faster than its trains did. Soon after this picture was taken, it was all over for the Penn Central. *Above:* A plethora of Conrail's EMD SD-40s. Diesel road switchers are the contemporary engine of choice.

diversify? Near the end of Symes' tenure, Symes had allied with the Madison Square Garden Corporation in the infamous project that demolished AJ Cassatt's monumental station.

Also at Symes' direction, old Broad Street Station in Philadelphia was razed to make way for the Penn Center complex of office buildings, apartments, garages, hotel, bus terminal and shopping center. In conjunction with a major realty company and the Chicago, Burlington & Quincy Railroad, Symes leased the air rights over several Pennsy Chicago properties, and an office complex was planned. The Pennsy's 11,000 acre holdings of undeveloped land were soon explored to reveal veins of coal and a salt deposit along the Ohio River.

In his tenure, Saunders sped things up a bit, even renegotiating the Chicago deal to create the framework for the present Gateway Center complex. Eventually, such Pennsy projects resulted ultimately in the remodeling of large portions of the downtown areas of several major cities. These projects would all bring home substantial returns—that was the hope of Pennsy management in the mid-1960s.

Saunders' expansive tendencies took root in the old Pennsylvania Company, which was instituted way back in 1870, to handle the Pennsy's western lines. Much of its interests were transferred to the parent company in

1918, leaving a bunch of securities which did nothing but gain interest over the years.

Saunders' first move in that direction was by way of buying out the Buckeye Pipeline Company—a dependable money earner, the eighth largest oil producer in the nation, and an important supplier of jet fuel. The initial purchase of 30 percent of the Buckeye's stock cost $28 million plus a new issue of preferred stock, and the closing purchases required more preferred stock and cash. Saunders soon thereafter bought a 60 percent interest in the Great Southwest Corporation, a land development operation specializing in theme amusement parks. Its flagship was Six Flags Over Texas, a huge amusement complex. Saunders bought 20 percent more stock in the company, and another huge theme park near Atlanta was planned—Six Flags Over Georgia. Another land-development corporation was bought into, the Arvida Corporation, a Florida enterprise specializing in retirement communities.

Saunders next acquired Macco Realty, a large residential real estate company; soon this holding too begat new, large, ambitious projects. The Strick Holding Company, which manufactured aluminum truck trailers, was the next Saunders acquisition.

All of these acquisitions were future-oriented save the Buckeye Pipeline Company. The Pennsy under Saunders was becoming one of the nation's leading land developers; it was becoming a company more interested in its investment portfolio than in railroading—good, some might say, the 'old fogeys' finally got the hang of it! There was a new mind at work in the Pennsy head of-

Tangled webs: The 3300 hp GE E33 electric road switcher shown *above* came to Conrail ranks via the Penn Central, which itself ingested this loco and nine of its brothers upon swallowing the New Haven, which in turn acquired the locos when it absorbed the Virginia Railway. Conrail has discontinued running most of its electrics.

fices...but not really. The essential fact of the Pennsy had always been that it would *grow*. From the first, the Pennsy was a formidable creature once it had a mind to acquire a holding, and it was this very fact that was proving to be its undoing. Alexander Cassatt's monumental coup in tunnelling to Manhattan and building a station there was that by doing it, the Pennsy garnered vast new passenger revenues, and greatly increased its business thereby. World War I struck an ominous note—too big was finally seen as a hindrance to operations; the Depression made tottering giants out of most railroads; World War II sounded a warning tocsin for overbuilding and the fifties clearly foretold the death of all uncontrollably big, unkempt operations.

The bold, terrible facts were that Saunders' regime had spent close to $200 million on these acquisitions, most of them based on futurity in an era that had proven so far to be unpredictable and highly unstable. The Pennsy had a big merger coming up, and cash reserves would be desperately needed.

Merger Complications

Furthermore, the ICC was yet to approve the merger—objections included charges of unfair competition with several very weak New England rail lines, the chief in-

valid among them being the New York, New Haven & Hartford. The NYNH&H had strong allies, including an army of New England congressmen and most of the members of the ICC.

The New Haven reported a deficit of $15 million in 1964—a deficit that would only rise, spectacularly, in the following years. The New Haven, knowing that a merger between the Pennsy and the NYC would spell doom for it, petitioned the ICC that the proposed merger include it as a party. Perlman and Saunders were not anxious to do this, but finally, seeing the merger postponed by several more years if this move were hotly contested, Saunders, over Perlman's objections, assented. This burden was compounded by worker organization demands.

It was felt, and rightly so, that the merger would result in further reductions in the companies' payrolls as management proceeded to slash away at redundant facilities and operations. Again over Perlman's objections, Saunders offered a lifetime pension to any worker employed at the time of the merger; any employee dismissed in the interim between the discussions and the merger had a right to be rehired, and all those fired with and without cause would receive a year's severance pay.

The unions in turn agreed that the roads' work force could be reduced by 5 percent per year—and no more—and that workers could be transferred, upon their agreement to do so, to new positions provided that the company pay moving expenses. This whole tangled mess was entitled the Merger Protective Agreement. It assailed Perlman's dream of having a tight, spare and efficient operation, and favored Saunders' sprawling conglomerate projections. This was a fundamental issue, no doubt about it, and the major parties in the upcoming merger were at bitter odds about it.

Forward to Disaster

There was nothing Perlman and the NYC management could do about it, lacking funds to move out on their own, and Saunders, much as he may actually have felt comfortable with the setup, was literally locked into conglomeracy by dint of the hefty worker assurances he had made, and by the many expenditures he had made in past years—the only direction was forward, to disaster.

This setup was very much the nature of the final merger product—riddled with deficits and a schizophrenic management, the giant, to whose existence objections had been raised concerning the raw power such a merger would represent, ducked and dodged about like a drunken sailor who has spent all his money one forgetful night before homecoming. It was a disaster, a mess riddled with such pettiness as the logo on the Penn Central's first annual report, which read '121st Annual Report'—literally as if the merger were a mere absorption of the NYC and the New Haven by the Pennsy! This dateline would give the new company's inception as the day the Pennsy first obtained its charter. In lieu of the careful expansion that tradition had dictated—care and upkeep of operations being the foundation of all previous expansion—the new organization was based on a three-part schism that merely looked cohesive from the outside; its main theme was conglomeration based on the very 'spacey' business climate of the times.

The Penn Central's three tiers of management were the Penn Central Transportation Company, which owned and operated the corporation's railroad operations and managed all railroad properties; the old Pennsylvania Company, basically a holding company; and the acquired one-railroad operations discussed earlier in this chapter, which were in effect owned and operated by the Pennsylvania Company.

To make a sad story short, the difficulties described in the preceding paragraphs—lack of care of railroad operations, animosities on the part of the major parties in the merger, and a somewhat uncautious approach to 'miracle' problem-solving (Saunders' expansive plans for making railroad operations finally just another holding in a projected huge conglomerate fell through with the recession of the late 1960s and early 1970s)—effectively destroyed the Penn Central.

A brief history of the company follows:

The merger was official on 1 February 1968. The full name of the new entity was the Pennsylvania New York Transportation Company. This was changed to 'Penn Central' on 8 May 1968, and on 1 October 1969, changed again to Penn Central Transportation Company, which became a wholly-owned subsidiary of the Penn Central Company, a holding company in line with Saunders' plans. Perlman was relegated to transportation operations, as was the entire former NYC crew, and all else in the new corporation was run out of Saunders' Philadelphia offices. Animosities continued, resulting in

Perlman's resignation in 1969. Perlman, as nominal 'president' of Penn Central, had been systematically replacing Pennsy railroad personnel with NYC personnel in the railroad ops, claiming that the Pennsy folks were used to running a loose ship, which was comparatively true, as the NYC had built its own business on manufactured goods which demanded exacting delivery times, and the Pennsy freight business was built on ore and coal, which were much less 'scheduling intensive.' The difference in procedures resulted in lost shipments, huge delays and a general breakdown of any such efficiency as either company had had before the merger.

This combined with in the late 1960s and early 1970s to cost the new company millions in freight business. Trucks were taking over Penn Central's dissatisfied customers. The amusement parks and some other real estate holdings were sold in 1969 as a monetary cover-up procedure for the company's ailing health.

Perlman resigned in anger at being refused a huge allocation for improvements. Perlman's position was filled by Paul Gorman, a retired president of Western Electric Company—who knew nothing of railroading.

The few years of the Penn Central's existence saw snafu after snafu, each one floated atop a witching patina of Saunders' glowing statements concerning the future of the company. With a little doctoring of the books, and some severe understatement in the yearly letter from the board, it was made to appear viable. But the truth was that in its first year, Penn Central lost $2.8 million; in 1969, $83 million; and in 1970, $325.8 million. On 21 June 1970, the product of the largest corporate merger in US history (to the date of its own inception) entered bankruptcy proceedings.

Its passenger operations, including the popular *Metroliner* high speed train from Washington to New York, were taken over by Amtrak on 1 May 1971.

The Mists of Creation

Despite the blunders and outright fraudulent behavior of Penn Central's management, mere human perfidy did not destroy the Pennsy or the Penn Central. The indifference of Congress, the ICC and the general public did much to contribute to the ruin of not only these but of many American railroads in the 1960s and 1970s. Railroads were forced to carry passengers at a less than 'break even' rate; competing modes of transportation were heavily subsidized; and unfriendly attitudes—both on the part of private citizens and on the part of legislators—had been formed about the railroads based upon popular myths that had lost currency decades before the Penn Central collapse.

On the part of the railroads, there was a sense of history; in the case of the NYC, this sense operated to urge modernization—meaning by this what it had always meant to railroads; running a tight operation—on the part of the Pennsy, it had somehow become ingrown, resulting in a nostalgia for the good old days, and a stubbornness about procedures that were no longer productive. In a sense, given that its hands were tied in terms of cutting back, the Pennsy lost momentum and fell into a kind of 'sloth.'

The Penn Central's collapse became an emblem of the

woes of an age. As the economic tide went in the 1950s and 1960s, so went the fortunes of the Pennsy, the NYC and, eventually, the Penn Central.

The Penn Central's collapse could have easily sparked a panic of the severity of the Crash of 1929; it didn't. The very bonds of necessity that held the railroads to unprofitable but essential passenger operations also kept the Penn Central afloat for awhile. The sheer necessity of maintaining operations of the US' number one military supply carrier resulted in a 'ward of court' status for the feeble giant. Several options were suggested for the remedy of the predicament. One was that the Perlman plan for operationally 'cleaning house' be adopted, with a whole new management team. This was done, and the road continued to lose tremendous sums of money. The fact was that the nation's industrial Northeast was depressed— rail carriers in that part of the country were folding up like houses of cards.

As far as passenger travel was concerned, the nationalized rail carrier, Amtrak, was losing money regularly, with estimated losses of $75 million per year, even if every available seat was 'paid up.'

This situation saw much legislation and even municipal action undertaken, including the leasing of Penn Central trackage for state-funded commuter lines in New York, Connecticut and Pennsylvania. Amtrak itself would rise to account for half of the nation's total rail passenger miles, and now operates over a 25,000-mile system. At one point, Amtrak resurrected, after an austere fashion, the famed New York-Chicago runs of the *20th Century Limited* and the *Broadway Limited.*

Above: These Conrail General Electric diesels are hustling an intermodal 'piggyback' trailer train through the countryside at Leetsdale, Pennsylvania. *Above right:* A safety cab passenger diesel leads Amtrak's *Superliner* in Illinois. *Opposite:* Amtrak continues the very popular *Metroliner* interurban commuter service.

The train would take the *20th Century's* 'water level' route, but would consist only of an engine, three coaches, one sleeper, one diner and a baggage car. Though it made the trip in the same time as the original, it was not a money-making proposition— unlike the profitable New York to Washington *Metroliner* service, taken over and continued by Amtrak, which even cut deeply into air travel over the same route. Still, Amtrak lost money, and made clear the need for government subsidizing of rail passenger travel.

With Penn Central's losses under new, 'clean' conditions, it became clear to everyone concerned that the operation would have had to fold up under any but the most optimal of conditions, mismanagement or no. In March 1973, the trustees of the corporation told federal judge John Fullam that their position had become untenable, that the Penn Central could go on no more; the line was but a breath away from total insolvency.

Despite many warning signals that this was inevitable, sluggish legislative response to the original Penn Central bankruptcy had allowed a bad situation to deteriorate further. Judge Fullam told the trustees that they were to cease all railroad operations by October 1 of that year, and then to proceed speedily with liquidation of all Penn Central assets, unless the government stepped in.

A nationalization bill was hastily prepared by Congress for introduction in the House, as this ultimatum awakened legislators to the seriousness of the situation. The Association of American Railroads did not want nationalization, and introduced their own solution at a special hearing. This solution was a slight modification of a proposal made by William McDonald and Frank Barnett—the vice president and chairman, respectively, of the Union Pacific. This proposal was that the bankrupt lines might be gathered under an umbrella entity from which they could sell bonds with government support, which revenues could be used to chop, cut, improve and generally make their moribund operations viable. The McDonald-Barnett solution would produce no profit-making wonders, but at least would put roads on an equal footing—in the private sector, where pork-barreling would also be reduced to a minimum (as the roads would, be forced to attempt honest operability).

After some debate, the AAR successfully championed its cause through Representative Dick Shoup of Montana. The chairman of the House subcommittee then reviewing the northeastern railroads' dilemma was Representative Brock Adams of Washington. Adams was not for nationalization, either, but was wary of the AAR's proposal. As Judge Fullam's deadline neared, however, Adams decided on the lesser—to him—of two evils, and joined Shoup in pushing the plan, which became known as the Shoup-Adams bill. Judge Fullam was satisfied that a plan was arrived at, and the Penn Central somehow made it through the autumn.

President Nixon, then embroiled in the Watergate fiasco, vowed that he would veto the act because it was too costly. Shoup-Adams passed both the House and Senate in December, and became known as the Regional Rail Reorganization Act. Considering the wide support the measure had gotten in both houses of Congress, Nixon relented and reluctantly signed the measure into law on 2 January 1974.

Reorganization

The terms of the Reorganization Act brought to bear an entity known as the United States Railway Association, which was financed by a $1.5 billion issue of government bonds. 'Usury,' as the acronym was pronounced by many, was to be the rectifier of the Penn Central's woes. USRA was authorized to slice almost half of the 30,000 miles of lines that the road had in operation at that point—a move which, had it been allowed the individual railroads 20 years earlier, might have forestalled and perhaps prevented the Penn Central fiasco.

The Penn Central exists now solely as an organization dedicated to unsnarling the immense legal tangle produced by its own collapse.

Conrail

After this pruning was done, the consolidated property was to be turned over to a new rail organization, a privately owned company, which would be known as

Consolidated Rail Corporation—'Conrail.' Stockholders in the bankrupt companies were to turn their stock over to the new organization, and in return, they would receive stock in Conrail plus approximately $1 billion worth of government guaranteed bonds.

The unions had their say, of course, and a quarter of a billion dollars was set aside for laid-off workers' compensation—those with five or more years of service were to collect their working salaries until reaching age 65. This ridiculous magnaniminity naturally sparked new protests from the media, popular opinion was reinforced in its opinion of the nation's railroads as gigantic carpetbaggers living off the public one way or another, and so on. The entire Transportation Act was thought to be 'special interest socialism.'

Lawsuits filled the air—most were filed by irate Penn Central shareholders. Meanwhile, Penn Central's management did nothing to improve or even maintain their trackage and equipment. Despite all this Conrail did come into existence on 9 November 1975; the provisions of its being were that it would initially own all the rights of way used by Amtrak, and the rights to many of the Northeast's commuter lines. The new corporation would take over most of the Penn Central, Ann Arbor, Lehigh Valley, Reading, Central of New Jersey, Lehigh & Hudson River and a large chunk of the Erie Lackawanna.

Conrail would continue Usury's abandonment program, cutting 6000 additional miles of low-usage lines from its accumulated miles of track. The

Above: Three EMD road switchers haul a Conrail coal train through the Pennsylvania hills, on the same four-track bed that Pennsy trains once rode. *Above left:* One of Conrail's busy, rebuilt freight yards.

remainder of the Erie Lackawanna was, furthermore, to go to the Chessie System. Before it could actually effect any of these wonders, Conrail had to have control of the railroads, which were still tied up in Congressional debates as to Conrail's funding.

These debates were solved via compromise in late 1975, and the solution went before President Ford for signature. Like Nixon, he didn't want to spend that much money on railroads. The irony here is that there had been only one piece of truly pro-railroad legislation from World War II until the Penn Central's collapse—this had been a federal loan guarantee program for loans under $250 million. For the five years after the Penn Central's collapse, Amtrak alone required almost a billion dollars in loan guarantees and direct grants. Yet federal subsidies of non-railroad transportation for the period from 1952 to the mid-1970s was nearly six times this amount.

On 5 February President Ford capitulated and signed the bill into law. It would be known as the Railroad Revitalization and Regulatory Reform Act of 1976. This omnibus legislation provided a new finance committee for Conrail, consisting of the secretary of the treasury, the secretary of transportation and the chief executive officer of USRA. This committee oversaw the flow of funds into Conrail, and had veto power over any decisions by its board.

Conrail in Operation

Conrail commenced operation on 1 April 1976, with $2.1 billion received from USRA in return for its preferred stock and convertible debentures. The bankrupt northeastern rail lines turned over their railroading assets to Conrail, and received millions of shares of Conrail's common and junior preferred stock in return.

Among Conrail's various 'heirlooms' received from the legally tangled cobwebs of its ancestors was a billion-dollar lawsuit on the part of the Penn Central Institutional Investors Group, which included most of the creditor banks and insurance groups that had been involved with the Penn Central.

Conrail would be a vital component in the economic health of the Northeast—just as its predecessors were. With 100,000 workers it would help move 500,000 commuters and 160,000 carloads of freight per day, and would dominate rail transportation in the region.

Arthur Lewis, chairman of the USRA, felt that Conrail would lose $1 million per day in its first year, but would show a profit of close to $600 million by 1985. Everyone felt that the railroads in the Northeast would continue to be essential, no matter what—but this profit-showing as predicted was taken rather tongue-in-cheek.

Conrail recorded a $39 million profit in 1981—up from a $244 million deficit the year before. In its first nine months of operation, in 1976, Conrail lost $246 million, which figure climbed to $412 million in 1977, and $430 million in 1977, and dropped in 1978 to $221 million.

The years following 1981, to 1986, saw profits of 174, 313, 500, 442 and 431 million dollars, respectively.

From its commencement of operations on 1 April 1976 through 31 December 1986, Conrail made capital expenditures of approximately $5.8 billion to improve and revamp its rolling stock and trackage. The company operates a network of some 13,700 miles. Its 35,000 employees help to move its fleet of 2500 locomotives and 84,000 freight cars. Conrail's main freight customers are the chemical industry, automobile industry, coal and ore industries, and the intermodal freight business; none of these, which together made up some 77 percent of Conrail's 1986 revenues, account for less than 10 percent, nor more than 18 percent of said revenues. Conrail, as of this writing, is the principal railroad serving America's Northeast and Midwest freight markets.

Such a balanced customer structure lends security to such a massive operation. Furthermore, Conrail adopts the policy that a healthy customer is a good customer, and therefore constantly strives to help its customers to facilitate the movement of their products. For example, with such innovative practices as 'double stack' container trains, Conrail can move freight inbound from the Far East to New York up to two weeks faster than the steamship lines using the Panama Canal. Tight, conscientious, swift operations and upgraded equipment is the key here.

When Conrail began operations, it inherited a practically decrepit melange of ill-used, neglected and abused rail lines. In particular, what had been the Pennsy's trackage had fallen far away from the days when the Keystone road was 'the world's standard railroad.' The 'deferred maintenance' of World War II combined with the dark days of the Penn Central fiasco to produce concrete assets that had been allowed to deteriorate to the point that Conrail's first concerns were to bring such trackage and rolling stock up to the point that it could once again bear running at normal speed!

Goals that had been set for the road's first year rehabilitation efforts were 4.1 million ties replaced, 6910 miles of track resurfaced and the laying of 727 miles of continuously welded rail (less jar and jolt; less equipment repairs). Conrail responded to these goals by installing 4.6 million ties, resurfacing 8260 miles of track and laying 727 miles of continuously welded rail.

In 1983, Conrail was able to divest itself of its passenger carriage through the provisions of the Northeast Rail Service Act—'NERSA'—of 1981. Conrail transferred its passenger operations to various regional authorities and to Amtrak. Prior to that time, passenger service was run on a government reimbursement for costs basis. The divestment of these lines of service resulted in a further paring down of Conrail services, allowing the company to conduct business on a freight-only basis.

Computerization

Technological innovations such as Conrail's computer system allow improved vigilance on line performance— this was borne out in the recession of 1982, when overall revenues dropped by approximately $600 million from the year before. By diligent attention to the relationship of income to expenses on each segment of Conrail's huge operation, it was possible to still turn a respectable profit, thus showing that Conrail has a resiliency that was feared to have fled forever from roads operating in the Northeast.

Conrail's computer system includes over 300,000 miles of circuitry and more than 2700 computer terminals. One of the many systems managed by this technology is the Transportation Monitoring System, which keeps tabs on freight movements to given terminals, and includes the service of relaying their arrivals at key points en route.

Conrail's Resource Management System keeps records of individual cars, their contents and their destination. When the car reaches the yard, computers monitor the delivery time to the customer of the car's contents, or if it has farther to go, computers dispatch it on a train to its next scheduled stop. The Connection Monitoring System keeps track of the car's movements according to schedule.

Computerized Traffic Control systems allow the dispatcher to program the proper route for a train at a computer terminal. The computer sets the track switches along the way, and provides a color-coded 'route map' by which the dispatcher can follow the movements of the train. Advances to this system include a setup in which the computer can suggest to the dispatcher possible 'best route' choices by which to expedite freight. These sophisticated systems have been installed in the Newark, Indianapolis and Altoona dispatching offices.

Conrail shops are loaded with computerized and robotized systems, including cranes, welding machines and a parts shuttle that transfers needed parts from

storage to the work area. Once the locomotive is serviced, field personnel can determine where it will be needed by a glance at a computer printout.

Additional computer systems identify and locate overheated freight car wheel bearings—'hot boxes,' which can cause derailings—and dragging equipment, as well as aiding in the design of signaling equipment and circuitry.

The upshot of all this talk of specialized testing equipment and innovation is that, like the Pennsy in its healthy days, Conrail is very committed to exacting the best performance possible from its equipment. Take Conrail's locomotive power for instance; Conrail's 1350 road locomotives have a combined horsepower of 3.5 million. Conrail's new GE C39-8 and EMD SD-60 diesels are more efficient and more powerful than their older couterparts. This means that a 16-year-old EMD SD-40 model may haul 3333 tons of freight between Selkirk and Buffalo, but the newer model C39-8 can haul 4239 tons along the same route, making for an echoing of the days when the Pennsy increased its efficiency by building larger, stronger cars and locos with that relatively new railroading substance called 'steel.'

Locomotives

The newer locos can apply more of their weight toward actually pulling the train, due to design refinements;

and also better control adhesion of their wheels to the track, thus losing less pulling power overall. In 1986, Conrail added a total of 55 new locomotives to its fleet. Of these, 22 are 3900 horsepower C39-8s and three 3800 horsepower SD-60s. Both models are equipped with microprocessor controls, which automatically 'tune' the loco into its best operating mode. In addition, today's diesels have modularized electrical components which make for fast repairs by allowing the immediate replacement of ailing parts—thus greatly reducing locomotive 'down time.'

Conrail's Technical Services Laboratory in Altoona is conducting experiments to measure fuel efficiency as it pertains to the drawbar pull of diesels. Traditionally, diesel fuel efficiency is measured by the amount of electricity generated at the loco's dynamo per gallons of fuel consumed to generate the electricity. Drawbar tests were the standard used for steam locos—this is definitely a new 'wrinkle' with a *deja vu* quality it.

Business Structure

Conrail markets its freight service through four business groups based on the type of equipment used to haul various types of freight.These are *open top hopper cars* for coal, coke, iron ore, fluxing stone and aggregates; *covered hopper tank cars* for chemicals, petroleum products, grain and grain products, and non-

Above: This Conrail triple header freight is crossing America's longest railroad bridge— at Rockville, Pennsylvania. An earlier Rockville bridge (see pages 42-43) was built when the Pennsy was still in its glory. *Above left:* Conrail freight rides the rails— and will for many years.

metallic minerals; *automotive gondola flat cars* for auto parts, finished autos, steel products, scrap iron and steel, machinery and aluminum products; *boxcar intermodal* for forest products, foods, consumer goods, industrial manufacturers, piggyback service and trucking.

Conrail is dedicated to tradition. This is evident in its care of equipment, prudent operational strategies and in the naming of its facilities— the 'Big Four' yard outside of Indianapolis; the Sam Rea Car Repair Shop at Hollidaysburg; and more— and in its complete commitment to the furtherance of railroading as a vital, healthy industry.

Looking to the Future

By passage of the Northeast Rail Service Act of 1981, Congress mandated that the Department of Transportation (DOT) recommend to Congress a method of transferring the US government's 85 percent common stock interest in Conrail to the private sector. DOT indicated that it intended to maintain Conrail as a single entity in any such transfer. In 1983, Conrail met two NERSA-mandated profitability standards, and USRA also determined Conrail to be a profitable carrier.

After buyout bids and counterbids on the part of such organizations as the Norfolk Southern Corporation, an investor group headed by Morgan Stanley & Co, the investment banking firm of Allen & Co and Conrail Ac-

quisition Corp, the Conrail Privatization Act was enacted on 21 October 1986. This act directed that the federal government's 85 percent common stock interest be transferred to the private sector by means of a public offering; this resulted in the largest initial public stock offering in US history, on 26 March 1986.

Conrail's operations in 1986 showed a good profit. Going 'private,' however, means that the rail carrier will have to pay substantial tax increases. A factor operating in the road's favor is that Conrail's net operating loss and investment tax carryforwards have been canceled by special act passed into law with the stock offering— a clean slate, if you will.

The various changes brought about would essentially reduce a net income figure such as Conrail's 1986 posting— $431 million— to a sum about half that much— $208 million.

Since Conrail does seem to be earnest about operating efficiently as a railroad, has made good on its operations by showing a profit and has weathered some of the traditional railroad vagaries so far— the northeastern winter and its train-stopping snows, slowdown of freight orders, economic slump and etc— there is an air of optimism about this 'phoenix' rising from the ashes.

INDEX